THE HOUSE OF HORROR:
The Complete Story of Hammer Films

Lorrimer

**Edited by Allen Eyles, Robert Adkinson
and Nicholas Fry**

Designed by Peter Warne & Associates

© 1973 Lorrimer Publishing Limited
First published 1973
Second printing 1974
Reprinted 1975
Second edition published 1981
Reprinted 1984

Enquiries should be addressed to Lorrimer Publishing Limited,
47 Dean Street, London W1V 5HL

Typeset in Baskerville by Dahling Dahling, London
Printed and bound by Interprint Limited,
Industrial Estate, Marsa, Malta.

The House of horror.—2nd ed.
  1. Hammer Film Productions
  2. Horror films—History and criticism
I. Eyles, Allen   II. Adkinson, Robert
III. Fry, Nicholas
791.43'75   PN1999.H3

ISBN 0-85647-115-1

THE HOUSE OF HORROR

The Devil Rides Out: Charles Gray, Nike Arrighi.

CONTENTS

There is an 8-page colour section of special Hammer publicity hand-outs between pages 64-65.

ACKNOWLEDGEMENTS

The publishers and editors wish to extend their deepest thanks to all the people and organisations who have made the compilation of this book possible.

Especial thanks are due to Mr. Michael Carreras, Mr. Terence Fisher, Mr. Christopher Lee and Mr. Peter Cushing, for allowing themselves to be interviewed; to Miss Jean Garioch, Mr. Anthony Carreras and Mr. K.F. Matthews, for their indefatigable help in compiling and producing the book; to Barbara de Lord, Carol Futrall and Graham Smith, for their help in making stills available for reproduction.

Our thanks are also due to the following distribution companies who have granted us permission to use stills from the Hammer films distributed by them (details of the films and companies are included in the Filmography): Rank Film Distributors, Columbia-Warner, MGM-EMI, and Cinema International Corporation.

FOUR VOICES FROM THE HOUSE OF HORROR

Michael Carreras

With 140 pictures produced in the past 25 years, Hammer Film Productions rates as one of the most successful and prolific film production companies in the world. While the present company was formed in 1947, the real origins of Hammer lie very much further in the past, when a Spaniard named Enrique Carreras bought his first cinema in Hammersmith, London, in 1913. Gradually building up a chain of cinemas, Enrique Carreras then went into partnership with one William Hinds, who worked in amateur variety under the stage name of Will Hammer, and the two of them formed a film distribution company — Exclusive Films Ltd. — in 1935. At the same time the next generation of the Carreras family, Enrique's son James (now Sir James Carreras, MBE), joined the company, to be followed by his own son, Michael, eight years later. It was from this company that Hammer Films eventually developed.

Michael Carreras became the managing director of Hammer in January 1971. As the third generation of the Carreras family to be involved in the operation, he has a unique perspective of Hammer's past development, and he is also the man on whom Hammer's future depends. Here he talks about the early days and the personalities of Exclusive's founders, Enrique Carreras and Will Hammer.

"My grandfather was a Spaniard; he came over from Spain, and my grandmother hardly learned to speak English to the day she died. They came from the same family as the tobacco firm, and it was his uncle or great uncle who finally severed the connection by selling out. My grandfather had been in many ventures in this country, including one misadventure with a new toothpaste which made him bankrupt. Eventually he drifted into the cinema exhibition side and built up an original chain of cinemas called the Blue Halls. As a matter of interest, in the early days of his exhibiting life my grandfather had the distinction of putting on the first Royal Command Performance ever. He rented the original *Ben Hur* film, rented the Albert Hall and invited royalty, and that was the first Royal Command performance.

"Parallel with that you have a man called Will Hinds or Hammer, who had many wide interests — including Hinds the jewellers, and some bicycle shops,

I believe. Eventually their paths crossed and they came together, by which time my grandfather was running a company called Exclusive Films, a very small distribution setup dealing only with reissue pictures and that sort of thing.

"The two of them had one thing in common. They were both very shy and retiring people. My grandfather carried much of the Spanish heritage with him, he was a very gentle man, much admired and liked. At the same time he was a very astute business man, and handled his affairs with a great deal of charm. All my images of him are as a very soft, kind man.

"Will Hinds, or Hammer, was also a very quiet and retiring man, but obviously had an extraordinary introverted desire to become extravert, because one of his great activities, both business-wise and as an active amateur, was theatricals. He had a theatrical agency, which employed a number of music-hall artists, he used to rent and own a number of seaside theatres which put on summer shows, and he himself liked to perform as a comedian. I never saw him do it professionally, but in those days when we were a distribution company as well we used to have a staff of about 130, and every year we used to have a staff outing. We would get on a coach and go down to Hastings or Southend or somewhere, and at the end of the lunch he always used to love to stand up and give us a performance. But this was totally in contrast to the character and personality of the man I actually knew."

While James Carreras was away in the Army (from 1939 to 1946), Michael Carreras had joined Exclusive Films in a junior capacity in 1943, the start of a long career in the family business:

"I had the advantage of going through all the various departments —

logging, buying, accounts — ending up in the publicity department, which was responsible for sending out the stills and the posters to the cinemas that were playing the various Exclusive releases. That was during the war, and we were in Wardour Street. I remember that the secretary of the company was a woman, who had a dog and insisted on bringing it to the office every day. So it was part of my job to walk down seven flights of stairs with this dog four times a day, at the same time as the doodle-bugs were dropping. It was a fairly exciting period . . ."

Exclusive Films continued in business in a limited way until the end of the Second World War, and began to produce a handful of films. As James Carreras was demobbed in 1946, so his son Michael began his military service in the Grenadier Guards. On returning to civilian life, James Carreras sought the advice of Jack Goodlatte, at that time booking manager for ABC cinemas: "He advised me to continue to produce low budget British films. I acted on that advice and the first film we made was entitled *River Patrol*."

In 1947, Hammer Films was formed to implement the production programme. At the same time, the younger generation of Hinds and Carreras returned from the Services, and both Michael Carreras and Will Hinds' son Tony started in the production side of the new company.

"I had for a short time been on the booking side of Exclusive Films," recalls Tony Hinds, "but after the war it took some persuasion from Sir James to talk me into rejoining the new Hammer company. I wanted to be a writer — not a producer and not necessarily in films at all. I started as general 'dog's body' and worked my way up, eventually realising my original ambition by writing scripts."

In 1951, Hammer Films joined

forces with the American production company, Robert Lippert Productions, and this move gave them their first foothold in the United States. While Michael Carreras produced a number of films which starred American artists under the new American co-production deal, his father was gradually building up the company's reputation abroad. As Michael Carreras says, his father provided a marked contrast to the older generation:

"He is a salesman par excellence, a man who as they say could sell refrigerators to eskimoes, and he has a tremendous outgoing personality. When I was a child, I think a lot of my energy was drained by just watching my father perform. He was a great sportsman, a great cricketer, a great rugby football player — never used to stop. He also loves social occasions and is at ease in any class of society or size of group. This is illustrated very much by his activities in the Variety Club, which developed later. He has become the international chairman and travels all over the world; he meets everybody and handles it all as to the manner born. He's an incredible extravert as opposed to the older generation.

"I think if we examine it very honestly those formative years under the guidance of, let's call them the elder statesmen, at least gave Hammer a firm footing, and a reputation within the film industry. An example is its relationship with the National Film Finance Corporation. A lot of people ended up owing them a great deal of money, but under the guidance of the elder statesmen we involved ourselves very heavily with the Film Finance Corporation and paid them back in full on the dates required. So a very good foundation was laid by then. Now in no way am I trying to take anything away from the expansiveness of Sir James Carreras,

but if he hadn't had an honest foundation to build upon, he really wouldn't have had the same success. By the same token, had Hammer Films not then inherited the services of Sir James Carreras, it would probably never have grown. So the two things are compatible and I think both must be recognised.

"The other thing that happened during the formative period is of course that both Tony and I learned our jobs. We neither of us knew anything, but we had the best possible schooling, because we were free to interfere in everything. I think we both had an enquiring mind, and we wanted to learn. We didn't accept the fact that we were producing pictures, we wanted to know how you photographed them, how you directed them, how you wrote them, how you cut them etc.; what happened in the laboratories, how you marketed and so on. So we had the tremendous advantage of having a kindergarten with all the toys available to play with and experiment with as we wished.

"Now during the period when neither of us knew anything Tony, who was older than I was, had the actual function of being the producer. I had the looser function of being assistant to him. I did casting for a time, I was story editor for a time, and almost anything else that amused me. Then after about the first three years of operation we shared the chore and alternated as producers. We were doing six pictures a year and Tony would do three, then I would do three, and that was the way it developed. Then we both took it in turns at various times in our history to become the executive producer. Our programme grew to about eight films a year and I was executive producer for a period of time, then I took an absence from Hammer and Tony became the executive producer. The other thing that he did do, interestingly, was to start writing, and he wrote a lot of horror films, in particular, under the name of John Elder."

It was in 1955 that the now steadily expanding company achieved its first major international success with *The Quatermass Xperiment*, released in the United States as *The Creeping Unknown*. The idea of a recognisably human monster had caught the public imagination, and Hammer decided to exploit the trend, first of all by reviving the Frankenstein and Dracula stories which had first been seen in the American horror films of the thirties. The first was *The Curse of Frankenstein*, made in 1956, which was directed by Terence Fisher, scripted by Tony Hinds under his pseudonym of John Elder, and starred a relatively unknown actor, Peter Cushing. The first *Dracula* followed in 1957, again directed by Terence Fisher, and launched another actor, Christopher Lee, to stardom. These two films remain Hammer's biggest successes, having grossed some £4 million between them, and started the trend which has made Hammer's name synonymous with horror throughout the world. By early 1960, Hammer had completed *Revenge of Frankenstein* and *Brides of Dracula* as the second in a whole series of Dracula and Frankenstein films which remain firm favourites up to the present day.

In 1961, Michael Carreras broke away from Hammer to form his own production company, Capricorn Films:

"The reason I broke away was that I wanted — like I think everyone does at some point — just to have a fresh scene. I didn't want to leave the industry or anything, but I wanted to try other facets. I wanted to make a different type of film, which I did immediately — a musical called *What a Crazy World*, which I co-wrote and directed, and then a Western called *The Savage Guns*, which as a matter of interest was the very first Western to be made in Almeria in Spain. I wanted to experiment in different types of subject because there was a very rigid pattern at Hammer at the time — a successful pattern but nevertheless a rigid one. By the same token, I wanted to gather a wider experience so that when I rejoined Hammer, which I always expected to do, it being a family concern, I would be able to bring this experience with me.

"Since both Tony Hinds and myself were capable of fulfilling the same function at Hammer, I think it was only a question of time as to whether it was I or Tony who went. In fact he also felt this psychological need and prior to my leaving he took a year off, and applied to the Union to be able to work in a much more lowly position, to gather experience. The Union refused him a ticket, and I think this is something they should be totally ashamed of, since he was a director and shareholder of a company which was probably giving more employment to British technicians than any other company.

"Tony Hinds eventually retired and sold out from what had been very much a two-family venture. My grandfather died first, then Tony's father, and then Tony himself decided to retire, for reasons which must be purely personal to him, I suppose. I don't think there's any other word for it, because as far as I know, since leaving Hammer he has done no more than write a couple of scripts and literally does lead the life of a retired gentleman."

During his formal absence from Hammer, Michael Carreras continued to produce individual pictures for the company, which was maintaining a steady output not only of horror films, but also comedies, thrillers, TV "spin-offs" and prehistoric subjects.

"I produced all the different kinds

of pictures that Hammer made — there was the Rider Haggard adventure, *She*, for instance, then *One Million Years BC* and *Moon Zero Two*, which were all different. I had never really lost close contact, and had probably been as much involved as anyone with their diversification of projects. This was what I wanted to achieve anyhow, but it worked better this way for me personally than it would have within the firm."

During the 'sixties, Hammer tied in with most of the major American distribution companies, such as Columbia, Warner and Fox, and in 1968 they received the Queen's Award to Industry after three years of production in which they had brought £1,500,000 in dollars into the UK per year. Their peak production was in 1971, with ten films completed within the twelve months. It was to this increasingly successful company that Michael Carreras finally returned in a formal capacity in 1971:

"The last thing I did while I was still acting independently was to make a picture in South Africa, which I both wrote and produced. That really took a year out of my life, during which I only came back to London once for three days. When I finally got back my father said to me laughingly, 'I suppose you've stopped buggering about now,' meaning that I ought to settle down. The first offer he made was that I should come back as executive producer. At that time they were still maintaining their output of eight pictures a year and I had no hesitation in saying no, because I would have been back exactly where I was when I left. I was suddenly being asked to take the responsibility for seven or eight other producers, which was the one thing which, if you like, I ran away from or didn't want to know about ten years previously. Also I was capable of earning a year's salary by producing one picture which I wanted

to do independently, without this responsibility. So I refused, which I think rather upset him. There was a brief pause and I didn't know whether I was ever going to hear from him again. Then just before Christmas of 1970 I was invited to come and have dinner in London, which I did. He asked me whether I would rejoin the company as managing director, which was a different proposition altogether. After thinking about it over Christmas I said yes, and rejoined the company full time on 3rd January 1971.

"To bring the story up to date, in August 1972 there were certain moves made to acquire this company by outside interests. By this time my father was nearing 65, and I think that he felt that he had taken Hammer as far as he and it could go. At any rate, in August 1972 I actually purchased the company from him.

"Up to that point, of course, the company had been run as a family business. Now although family businesses are a wonderful way of life, I don't think they exist today in the same way as they did in the past, and I believe that Hammer has a potential diversify into other compatible areas. For instance, immediately I think of bookshops — the name Hammer would be acceptable on a certain type of book as it is on a certain type of film. I think of the record world, and I would like to go into a West End grand-guignol theatre—restaurant—late night movie house—museum complex. I think of the name Hammer Entertainment in that style. There are a lot of developments I want to do, and so as from August 1972 my position has really been that of major shareholder, chairman, managing director, executive producer and everything else. Again, this is only a temporary situation because, without losing any of the image, I want to reshape the structure of the company, build it towards an aim and diversify its activities. I've got a sort of five-year plan in my mind.

"As to the question of whether another generation of the Carreras family will be involved with the company — I have three sons. The eldest is now 23; he is in the film business, but he doesn't like to work for Hammer; he works as an assistant director, as a freelance technician. My middle son is studying interior design, and he's just 21. He could go into art direction if you like, but he may not want to. And my youngest son, who is 19, joined me here in January 1973; I hope to be able to give him the opportunity of seeing as many facets of the business as possible, in case he should decide to go into it. So I've got three possibilities . . ."

Terence Fisher

Doyen of all contemporary fantasy film directors, creator of the first and most famous films in the Hammer Dracula and Frankenstein series and director of many of the company's more notable successes since, is Terence Fisher. His first film for Hammer, *The Last Page*, was made in 1951, and between then and the first *Frankenstein* (1956), he made a number of very successful features for the company, including *Stolen Face, Mantrap, The Four-sided Triangle, Spaceways, Blood Orange, Face the Music, Mask of Dust,* and *Men of Sherwood Forest*. When, in 1956, Hammer took the decision to remake the famous Hollywood horror movies

of the 'thirties, it was Terence Fisher who was chosen to direct the first one, *The Curse of Frankenstein*.

The film was an immediate commercial success and it has recouped something in the region of five million dollars worldwide; it also established Terence Fisher as a master of the horror and fantasy genre, a position confirmed in 1957, when he directed the first Hammer *Dracula*. Since these first two films Terence Fisher has directed numerous sequels to them, though not all the subsequent Hammer Frankenstein and Dracula films have been directed by him.

Fisher, though, has never confined himself solely to the Dracula and

Frankenstein themes, although he admits that he prefers making these films to any others. In 1958 he directed *Hound of the Baskervilles* and *The Man Who Could Cheat Death*. In 1959 came *The Mummy, Stranglers of Bombay* and *The Two Faces of Dr. Jekyll*. The 'sixties saw the making of more varied features, including *Phantom of the Opera* and *The Devil Rides Out* and the continuation of the Frankenstein and Dracula films, culminating in 1969 with *Frankenstein Must be Destroyed*, the year in which the first of two accidents occurred which were to keep Terence Fisher out of film-making for the best part of three years. On his return to film-making, the Master of the Macabre, as he has come to be known, went back immediately to his favourite theme with *Frankenstein and the Monster from Hell* (1973). But the first beginnings of Terence Fisher's working life were very different from the position he now occupies as the leading living cult director to the world's fantasy movie enthusiasts.

"My first career was my career at sea. I was an only child and, after my father's death in 1908, my mother thought that a period at sea would give some direction to my life; in fact, of course, it put me in the way of a great many temptations. After two years spent on a training ship, I finally went to sea when I was seventeen. It was a wonderful life for five or six years, but I never looked on it as an occupation for a lifetime.

"I can't remember having very definite ideas about what I wanted to do at this period. And my second, short, career was in the rag trade; I eventually became assistant display manager at Peter Jones. The only reason I can remember for working there was that we happened to live near the shop at the time."

It was during this period at Peter Jones that Terence Fisher first began to think of films as a possible career, though he recalls no specific event which turned him in this direction. A vague ambition to enter the film industry gradually crystallised into a more definite wish to become a film editor. And, at the relatively advanced age of twenty-eight, he was accepted at Shepherd's Bush Studios, where he spent a year as "the oldest clapper-boy in the business." His next move was to the cutting room, where, after only nine months, he began cutting his own films, including a number of Will Hay comedies. Still a film editor, Terence Fisher then went to work at Teddington Studios, which were owned by Warner Brothers. The final step towards becoming a film director came in 1947, however, when he went to Highbury Studios at the invitation of the Rank Organization who were running a training scheme there for potential directors. After directing three short features, Sydney Box offered him his first full feature chance. "And that," says Terry Fisher, "was the start of it all."

"I made two films with Sydney Box at Pinewood. Then, of course, Rank began to be very wary about their investment in films and the whole industry in Britain began to go through a very bad time — apart from Hammer, who were applying themselves very seriously to improving their product. And so I joined Hammer.

"I distinctly remember the first film I made for them, *The Last Page* (1951), because of Diana Dors. She had been one of the Rank starlets and I can very well remember being impressed at the time by her great potential talent. I've never known her to give a bad performance, at least not when she was paying serious attention to her acting. None of these early films, though, really showed what my future career at Hammer was to be, apart perhaps from *The Four-sided Triangle*, which was science-fiction."

One of the turning points in the history of Hammer films and a considerable influence on Terence Fisher's later career was the success of Val Guest's *Quatermass Xperiment*. Not only was it one of the first television spin-offs, it also brought together those particular elements of fantasy and the macabre which were to make Hammer one of the most respected and profitable companies in the business. Hammer recognized in the success of Quatermass the great popular appeal of films dealing with horror and the unknown: the recognition of the potential of this combination was brilliantly embodied in the decision to resurrect the Frankenstein story. And Terence Fisher was to be the director of the first Hammer Frankenstein.

"Although I was absolutely delighted with the opportunity, I must admit that my being asked to direct the first *Frankenstein* was a stroke of pure luck. It happened that, under the terms of my contract, I was owed a film by Hammer, and the next one happened to be the *Frankenstein*. Hammer wanted me to see earlier film versions of the Frankenstein story, but I refused to do this, because I think everybody should bring his own individual approach to a subject, while remaining within the broader confines of the original story. I tried to forget the idea that I was continuing the central horror tradition of the cinema. I wanted the film to grow out of personal contact with the actors and out of the influence of the very special sets. I have never read Mary Shelley's original book, and I don't think I ought to read it. The greatest credit ought to go to Jimmy Sangster, who wrote the scripts and managed to make the original story so cinematic.

"Even when I came to shoot the Dracula films I still did not consult Bram Stoker's novels or the Transylvanian vampire legends. I think my greatest contribution to the Dracula myth was to bring out the underlying sexual element in the story. I also believe that the first Dracula film is just about the best thing I have ever done for Hammer, and it still looks a very successful film; everything seemed to hang together for once during the shooting. I remember Dracula's first appearance especially well. The boy standing in the hall of the house turns and looks up the staircase, and way up above is the figure of Dracula, silhouetted at the top of the stairs. The camera is shooting up towards this figure as he descends, still in silhouette, towards us. The audience expects the worst possible horror as he comes right up to the camera, then into view comes this very charming, handsome man. The shock effect is totally successful."

After the great commercial success of the first Frankenstein and Dracula films, which Terence Fisher suspected was possible, even before he had finished his first film in the series, Hammer have tended to give him almost exclusively the same kind of film to direct and many of these have been outside the Dracula/Frankenstein series, although he does admit that he prefers working with the two greatest and most popular Hammer "heroes". He also thinks that the two legends have an indefinite future on film since they are capable of assimilating all varieties of new ideas, such as the transplanting of brains, which occurs in *Frankenstein and the Monster from Hell*. He is not, however, very happy about the recent tendency to place Dracula in a modern setting.

"I think an audience has to find what it sees in the cinema absolutely convincing for the ninety minutes of the film. I don't really care what they think when they get out to the cinema, but unless they have believed in your film, you have not achieved your purpose. I would have no objection to doing a modern psychological thriller about vampirism, but why on earth have poor old Dracula trotting up and down the King's Road? You have to aim for a suspension of disbelief. Visually speaking, I think that my own films are good and believable, because I have a good visual sense within the frame. I hate what I call 'tricky shooting' — which makes a film look like a long TV commercial. This doesn't mean, though, that I don't approve of the use of special effects in the Frankenstein and Dracula films. In *Frankenstein and the Monster from Hell,* for instance, we have been able to show the whole of the brain transplant operation. You can actually see the top of the skull being taken off and the brain lifted out. But unless this sort of thing is done superbly, the effect is absolutely laughable.

"The real task of the fantasy film director is to bring integrity of intention to his film-making. I always ask for a similar response from my actors, and I rarely fail to get it, especially from Peter Cushing and Christopher Lee. If my films reflect my own personal view of the world in any way, it is in their showing of the ultimate victory of good over evil, in which I do believe. It may take human beings a long time to achieve this, but I do believe that this is how events work out in the end."

Christopher Lee

Christopher Lee is the greatest and most famous of all modern screen Draculas, a role he takes with great seriousness, showing impressive acquaintanceship with Bram Stoker's *Dracula* and the vampires of Transylvanian legend. He sometimes regrets that the Dracula he is asked to play on the screen is so far removed from the legendary and literary Draculas. But, as a professional actor, he interprets the roles he is given, and many of these have been outside the horror genre. Whatever part he is called upon to play, though, whether that of the evil Count or the pathetic Creature created by Baron von Frankenstein, Christopher Lee believes that it should be approached with total integrity: "One must immerse oneself completely in the character and forget one's own personality entirely. The portrayal from start to finish must be straight, honest and sincere. A trace of tongue-in-the-cheek deserves the audience's laughter."

Born in London in 1922, Christopher Lee went to work in business in the City of London after leaving school. On leaving the Royal Air Force at the end of World War II, he decided to become an actor, though he admits that he finds it difficult to remember why he took the decision to join the profession which was later to take him to the heights of international success. "I suppose it was just an urge to create people that weren't me," he says, "and because I felt I could do it better than anything else." At first the parts were small, but did include appearances in *Hamlet* and *Scott of the Antarctic*.

One of the great turning points in his career, however, undoubtedly came in 1956 when Hammer asked him to play the creature in their first remake of the great horror movies of the 'thirties, *The Curse of Frankenstein*.

"I was asked to play the creature chiefly because of my size and height," says six-foot five Lee, "which had effectively kept me out of many pictures I might have appeared in during the preceding ten years. Most British stars flatly refused to have me anywhere near them in a film, because I was easily the tallest man around. The tallest British star at the time was about six-foot two, and still shorter than me. So I spent those ten years learning the craft of acting. You can't learn how to be an actor, you have to learn how to act. I did television, theatre and opera during this period. In fact, everything I had done turned out to be a tremendous advantage for the role of the Creature; I had the necessary knowledge of mime because I'd never had the chance to say very much during the previous ten years, except when I went to make films in Europe.

"I've never really thought about what I would have done if the role of the Creature had not come along; I would probably have gone to America, where tall actors were very much in demand. Finally, though, the Hammer offer came along and my agent suggested I see Tony Hinds and Terence Fisher. I went along and

convinced them that I would make a suitable Creature, if only by virtue of my size. I didn't care if they made me totally unrecognizable; I wasn't getting anywhere looking like myself, so I thought that perhaps people would take a little more notice of me if I looked like nothing on earth. The result was the biggest grossing film in the history of the British cinema in relation to cost."

Christopher Lee's part in *Frankenstein* brought him into contact with another actor, Peter Cushing, with whom he was to establish an acting partnership which has ensured the continuing quality of the major Hammer fantasy films and has, indeed, proved to be the most notable twosome in the history of the horror genre. It would be untrue, however, to describe the great understanding between the two actors as a double act, since both of them have very active and varied film careers outside the Gothic revival movies they have made for Hammer.

After their outstanding success in the leading roles in the first Hammer remake, it was natural that the two men should come together again for the company's second, and equally successful, venture into fantasy, *Dracula* (1957).

This is a role which holds a special fascination for Christopher Lee and he is always very conscious of the vampire Count's historical and legendary antecedents whenever he is called upon to play the part. He has recently finished a documentary, shot on location in Rumania for a Swedish film company, in which he appears both as the fictional vampire Count Dracula and as the genuinely historical Vlad the Impaler, the fifteenth-century scourge of the Turks and the "real" Dracula. Lee does, however, have strong misgivings about the way in which he has been asked to play Dracula recently, and he tends to look back to the first Hammer *Dracula* with especial affection.

"With *Frankenstein* a proven success, I then played Dracula in the only version which Hammer have made that in any way resembles Bram Stoker's book. That was the first time I had played Dracula and in that film he did resemble Bram Stoker's creation in many ways, except in appearance, which was wrong and has remained wrong in every subsequent film version of the story. The Dracula of the book wore a coat, while all this business of cloaks and opera capes comes from the old Universal pictures. The idea of a man living in the depths of Transylvania, dressed up in white tie and tails and a cape is really quite ridiculous."

But, in spite of his misgivings about his screen Draculas, Christopher Lee's great triumph in the role has been to make the unbelievable believable. He projects the savage, erotic power of the creature whose continued exist-ence depends upon the draining away of life; and the Hammer *Draculas* have all underlined the power the Count has over his women victims. Lee also emphasises Dracula's vulnerability, the essential loneliness of evil.

"I think he's a very sad person. He's not a hero, but an anti-hero in many ways. He has tremendous ferocity and power, but he doesn't always have it under control. It is a difficult feat for an actor to make him believable; for an hour and a half the audience is looking at something they know can't happen and are believing that it can. I've often wondered what some of the greatest names in cinema would have made of some of the lines I have had to deliver; we at Hammer have had the most stringent training possible in this respect and we've come through with almost total success.

"Another aspect of these films which draws audiences to them everywhere is that the Dracula type of film is basically a morality play, with an admixture of pantomime, fairy story and melodrama. The characters are straightforward and strictly defined: this is black, this is white; this is good, this is bad. When evil meets good it must inevitably fall; it must always lose in the end. This is one reason why the church doesn't object to these films, and why they are so popular in Ireland, Spain and Italy. I have travelled all over the world and spoken to cinema-going people everywhere, and I have no doubt that, of all types of film, this type of fantasy or adult fairy-tale is the most popular."

Lee has, with Peter Cushing, been the leading star in the Hammer Gothic revival; he has played the creature in *Frankenstein*, Dracula and the Mummy. Now, in spite of his doubts about more recent ways of bringing the evil Count back to life, he is still generous in his praise of the company's achievement.

"There's no real difference between what Hammer makes and what a really large studio like Paramount makes, except that Hammer creates far more with far less. They manage to put on the screen a story, essentially unbelievable, which the actors then make believable, without spending absolute fortunes on script, direction and cast. Hammer is meeting a far greater challenge than many number one studio prestige productions, and winning hands down. The profits made by Hammer films leave no doubt about this. I think the critics are very unfair to Hammer; they criticize the films for being disgusting, shoddy and cheap. Yet there's more violence, sadism and obscene beast-liness in three minutes of a Bond film, than in twenty Hammer films combined.

"Hammer has never claimed to be here for anything other than to provide the general cinema-going public with the entertainment it wants. That, of course, is the job of a showman, and in the Carreras family we have had the best showmen in the British cinema for a very long time."

Christopher Lee's reluctance to go on playing Dracula as he has been characterised in recent Hammer films is perhaps understandable. Since the heady days of the first remake of 1957, subsequent versions of the story have tended to lose the mystery and fantasy of that first Terence Fisher *Dracula*, and have left Lee with little alternative but to go on playing the same screen Dracula, dressed in operatic cloak and glaring ferociously through red contact lenses. Lee, who usually carries a copy of Stoker's novel about with him on the Dracula sets, wants to see a return to the legend, both to Bram Stoker and the fifteenth-century legends.

"As the part has been envisaged in recent films, I feel there is very little on which I can elaborate. I am willing to play it again, but only if I feel there is something extra I can bring to it; and I do have reservations about playing the role in modern settings. Obviously, though, if the public wants to see me go on playing the part, then it becomes very difficult to refuse, although there will come a time when I shall no longer be physically capable of doing it. My ultimate ambition is to do a film of Stoker's book, as Stoker really wrote it. That's the Dracula I want to do. Then I could really say I'd played Dracula and bid a final good-bye to him."

Peter Cushing

Born in Surrey, England, in 1913, the son of a quantity surveyor, Peter

Cushing's persistent ambition, from his early days at school, was to be an actor. His father, however, had other ideas and Peter Cushing recalls, "I was an assistant in his office for three years and lived only for the evenings when I could rush off to the local amateur dramatic society." After a desperate period of writing secret letters of application to repertory companies and drama principals, the future Baron von Frankenstein finally got a job at fifteen shillings a week with the repertory company at Worthing. He stayed there until he had saved £50, the one-way fare to Hollywood.

After a varied two years in the United States, which included playing Louis Hayward's stunt man and double in *The Man in the Iron Mask* and a part in *Chumps at Oxford* with Laurel and Hardy, he returned to England in 1941. A long-standing ear complaint prevented his admission into an active branch of the Services, and he began to work with ENSA (Entertainments National Service Association). There were also various theatre appearances and an Old Vic tour of Australia and New Zealand. Then the first screen parts began to come, including that of Osric in the Olivier *Hamlet* of 1948. Other small film roles followed and, between 1951 and 1956, parts in no less than twenty-three television plays, including an award-winning performance in the adaptation of George Orwell's *1984*.

"I seemed to do nothing but plays then, wonderful plays. Practically every play I did in those years had already proved itself in the theatre — plays like *Gaslight* and *The Winslow Boy*. Every one was a winner and every part superb, which is a great help to any actor, because once you've got a good part in a good play you have to be very bad to fail. I do remember, though, that film people were very anti-television at the time."

One company, however, was fully alive to the extent to which radio and television represented popular taste. Hammer had already made spin-offs from popular radio programmes in the 'forties — the P.C.49 and Dick Barton films — when they launched their first, brilliantly successful, television spin-off, *The Quatermass Xperiment* (1955).

"I think this shows quite brilliant business acumen on the part of Hammer, but they have always watched television very closely, and now of course they're doing things like *On the Buses*, still with immense success. It was partly because of my success in television that Hammer approached me, but I couldn't begin working with them until 1956, when there was a slight lull in my television work, and I heard they were considering a remake of *Frankenstein*. I remember liking the earlier version very much, which had Boris Karloff playing the monster and Colin Clive playing Frankenstein. So I rang my agent, who told Hammer I was still keen to work for them. And that's how it all happened; I had no idea what I was beginning, though I soon found out that everything Christopher Lee and I did afterwards was described as a 'horror' film, even the Sherlock Holmes film I did. To me, though, it is films like *The Godfather* which are the real horror pictures, wonderful though they are. A man having his eyes shot out on a massage table parallels my driving a stake through Dracula, but it's really far more horrifying, because what we are enacting is really a fable, while the scene from *The Godfather* may really have happened at some time. I have no deep personal interest in the horror genre, but I do enjoy making films, and I feel extremely lucky to have been so closely associated with the Hammer success story. I have done an average of one and a half films a year for one company; in any actor's life, that is something to be deeply grateful for."

Peter Cushing, a gentle, quiet man in person, is renowned for playing two of the steeliest characters in the history of the horror film: the ruthless, fanatical scientist, Baron von Frankenstein, and the equally determined and fearless van Helsing, Dracula's perennial hunter. He has played these two parts in most of the Hammer treatments of the two stories, but he does not think the essential style of the characters has changed, in spite of a certain "modernisation".

"Frankenstein has tremendous style, because he is always the same character. He has perhaps become a little more ruthless, but basically he remains the same. The actor's character must always come through to a certain extent, which makes for some kind of continuity. You also try to create your character from what the scriptwriter has given you, and I don't think that Peter Cushing is all that much like Frankenstein. You are substantially governed by the script, and the way in which these are written is bound to reflect current attitudes to some extent.

"I don't, however, think that Frankenstein and Dracula have basically changed from the characters they were in the first films we made on those themes. *Frankenstein* is about a man who has done the impossible in creating another man; the other, *Dracula*, is about a vampire creature who lives on blood. Everything after that is a variation on the same theme. Of course you have to bring in changes somewhere, and Hammer have started to make Dracula films in modern settings, but the characters themselves remain very much the same. And, even in the modern version, Dracula himself is always kept within the confines of an old gothic church, where he is really at home.

"Nor does the way I imagine Frankenstein ever change. I think of him as being rather like Dr. Knox, the famous anatomist, who needed corpses to find out how the human body worked. He may have started out as an honest physician, but in the end he closed his one good eye to the means used to provide him with material for his experiments. And I see Frankenstein like that, not just as a man who collects bits and pieces to put together. He was really trying to prove something, and for that reason I have never thought of him as being an essentially bad character. Doctors and surgeons have always had to have a ruthless streak in them, in order to do their job."

Since making the first Hammer *Frankenstein*, Peter Cushing has starred in over fifty films. Many of those have come within the horror or fantasy category, like *Twins of Evil* and *The Creeping Flesh*. But after his characterisations of Frankenstein and van Helsing, he is probably best known for his playing of Sherlock Holmes, both in Hammer's *Hound of the Baskervilles* and for the very popular BBC television series. Peter Cushing remembers him as being "the most complex character to play." But Cushing's true affection still lies with the two film fantasies which have already assured him of a very distinguished place in the history of the horror genre.

"I hope Hammer have scripts ready for future *Dracula* and *Frankenstein* films which I can play in a wheelchair. The horror pictures give so much pleasure. And that is what film-making is all about. How lucky I was to get the first chance sixteen years ago.

"Give up playing van Helsing in the *Draculas*? Over my dead body."

HAMMER RIDES OUT

To every keen filmgoer, the word "Hammer" is synonymous with horror. But when Hammer made its name world famous with its new versions of *Frankenstein* and *Dracula* in the late 1950s, and started Peter Cushing and Christopher Lee on the road to becoming the latter-day equivalents of Karloff and Lugosi, it already had many years of film production behind it. Thus it had a solid foundation with which to follow up the new interest it had discovered in serious horror pictures, including a regular team of workers and an expert knowledge of economical production methods.

However, few people, even within Hammer itself, still recall that Hammer's experience in film production dates back to the 1930s, when a forerunner of the present company, also called Hammer, was briefly active in production. Behind the company then, as later, was Will Hammer, whose real name was William Hinds and whose son, Anthony, figures so importantly in the later, great success of the company. William Hinds was originally a businessman with a chain of jewellery shops who dabbled in amateur variety using the stage name of Will Hammer. He went into film distribution, forming a company called Exclusive with a cinema owner, Enrique Carreras, whose son James (now Sir James Carreras) and grandson Michael also have a major role in the eventual achievements of Hammer.

When Hammer Productions Ltd. was registered in November 1934, Will Hammer was Chairman; the joint managing directors were George A. Gillings and H. Fraser Passmore; while the other directors were George Mozart, who also acted in two of the company's productions, and J. Elder Wills, an established art director who actually directed two of the new company's pictures and later returned to film designing on many of Hammer's productions in the 1950s.

The first Hammer picture to come out was **The Public Life of Henry the Ninth** (1935), a comedy starring Leonard Henry as an unemployed London street entertainer who is engaged to perform in a public house where his success leads to a big stage break. The title, of course, was a shrewd, eye-catching variation on that of a celebrated historical film with Charles Laughton, and the film was polished enough to be distributed by Metro-Goldwyn-Mayer although its length (60 minutes) places it as a supporting feature. The second Hammer production was more ambitious: **The Mystery of the Marie Celeste** (1936). It seems to have been a lavish undertaking and it is interesting to find that, among those

The Mystery of the Marie Celeste:
Edmund Willard, Bela Lugosi.

involved in this particular explanation of a celebrated maritime mystery was none other that the former Count Dracula, Bela Lugosi, ensuring the film its American release under the title *The Phantom Ship*.

Then Hammer made **The Song of Freedom** (1936) with Paul Robeson,

Song of Freedom: Paul Robeson.

fresh from his success in *Sanders of the River* and here playing the African slave who becomes a well-known popular singer and returns to his native land to save his people from the power of the witch doctors. Will Hammer himself, as well as George Mozart, appeared in a supporting role. Next came **Sporting Love** (1937), a farce with a racing background adapted from the stage hit by Stanley Lupino and starring its author and Laddie Cliff as two brothers in "a continual trough of financial depression". After this there is no trace of further Hammer productions, and by the time the Second World War broke out it was no longer listed as an active British film-making company.

These early productions, however, saw a new lease of life when they were reissued by Exclusive, although they had been handled originally by other, bigger distributors. And when the company was encouraged by the ABC cinema circuit to supply low-budget British supporting features after the war, this was the impetus for re-forming Hammer in 1947 as a producing subsidiary of Exclusive, to supplement the films it was receiving from British independent producers like Henry Halsted's Marylebone Studios. (The present Hammer company was not actually registered until February 1949. It was titled Hammer Film Productions Ltd., with William Hinds (Will Hammer), Enrique Carreras, James Carreras and Anthony Hinds as directors. Today its directors are Michael Carreras and Brian Lawrence.)

The first result was a modest 46 minute thriller, **River Patrol** (1948), a Hammer-Knightsbridge co-production about a young customs agent rounding up a gang of nylon smugglers. This was followed by the more ambitious **Dick Barton, Special Agent** (1948), co-produced with Marylebone and based on the appeal of the radio series of Barton adventures. Here Dick Barton (Don Stannard) took a holiday at a small

Dick Barton, Special Agent:
Don Stannard, Arthur Bush

fishing village and foiled the plans of a fanatic to pollute Britain's water supply with deadly germ bombs. This was well enough received to lead to **Dick Barton Strikes Back** (1950, Barton versus international criminals with atomic weapons), which seems to have been produced by Exclusive itself rather than Hammer, and **Dick Barton at Bay** (1950), a Hammer production with Barton rescuing a British scientist, inventor of a death ray, from the clutches of a foreign agent who is holding him captive in the lighthouse at Beachy Head. The series would probably have been extended had not its star, Don Stannard, died in a car crash.

British radio programmes also furnished the idea for other productions of this period by Hammer and Exclusive. There were two stories concerning Archibald Berkeley Willoughby, P.C. 49; **Celia**, a comedy

Room to Let: Valentine Dyall.

A Case for P.C. 49: Brian Reece.

thriller with a woman crime investigator; **The Man in Black**, with Valentine Dyall telling the story of two villainesses; and **Meet Simon Cherry**, with a Reverend doing the sleuthing. There was also an interesting hint of Hammer's future path to

success in **Room to Let** (1950), from a BBC play by Margery Allingham, with echoes of Marie Belloc Lowndes' *The Lodger* in its story of a Victorian family who believe that their lodger, the sinister Dr. Fell (Valentine Dyall), may be Jack the Ripper.

Other productions with conventional comedy, crime, and romantic elements were made, many of them from stage plays, but these also were programme fillers with minor British stars and negligible appeal on the vast American market (although most of them were used to feed the voracious appetite of American television). The first film to be specifically geared for widespread American acceptance was **Cloudburst** (1951) with a well-known Hollywood actor, Robert Preston, in the leading role. It was made by Hammer, the first film to be shot at the company's new Bray Studios at Windsor (a converted private house), and it was released in the States by United Artists. The rest of the cast was British and the film used a fairly common device of making Preston's character into a Canadian to make him more acceptable to British audiences. Preston was one of the most talented actors that Hammer-Exclusive imported and the film had the fortunate side-effect that Preston was so struck by the stage training and concurrent stage work of his fellow players that it helped influence him to return to the American stage, where he had the success that brought him back to the major roles in Hollywood. In *Cloudburst* he was an intelligence officer working at the Foreign Office who tracks down and kills two criminals who have accidentally killed his pregnant wife. He then attempts to commit suicide and is left to contemplate the futility of personal revenge. It was sombre stuff compared to the films that followed.

The great advantage that British film producers had at this time was that they could supply at reasonable cost the kind of modest B picture that was fast dying out in Hollywood due to rising costs and a shrinking market. Thus Hammer were able to star American actor Richard Carlson in **Whispering Smith Hits London** (1952) and provide RKO Radio with an acceptable picture for their American release schedules. When RKO decided to revive its series of Saint adventures in the following year, it arranged for Hammer to produce the film (called **The Saint's Return** in Britain, *The Saint's Girl Friday* in America) and dispatched Louis Hayward to portray Leslie Charteris's sleuth, Simon Templar, as he had done in RKO's very first Saint film, *The Saint in New York*, back in 1938.

However, the British company's main co-production link was with an American producer-distributor, Robert L. Lippert. It had the added advantage that Exclusive distributed Lippert's American productions, considerably augmenting the number of films it released. On the production side, well over a dozen films were made by Hammer and Exclusive, using American stars, an occasional American director (Sam Newfield), and frequently involving Lippert's American writers, notably Richard Landau. The first co-production was **The Last Page** (retitled *Man Bait* by Lippert) in which George Brent,

The Last Page: Diana Dors, George Brent.

nearing the end of his career, portrays a London bookshop manager blackmailed by Diana Dors as his busty young assistant in cahoots with her boyfriend (Peter Reynolds). Another American star, Marguerite Chapman, provided the conventional love interest for a happy ending. Terence Fisher was the director (his first work for Hammer-Exclusive); Frederick Knott, better known as the author of *Dial M for Murder* did the screenplay from a stage play by James Hadley Chase. All told, far more striking talents were at work than on any previous Hammer picture, and commercially it did the trick. Terence Fisher continued with a minor smuggling drama, **Wings of Danger** (1952) with Zachary Scott, then directed Paul Henreid and Lizabeth Scott in **Stolen Face** (also 1952). In

Stolen Face: Paul Henreid, Mary Mackenzie.

the Harley Street plastic surgeon played by Henreid this film has a prototype of the kind of demented scientist-doctor that would crop up in Hammer's later genuine horror films. Here, when the surgeon loses his girlfriend (Lizabeth Scott), he is so distraught that he sets about modelling the face of a patient, a criminal psychopath (Mary Mackenzie), into an exact replica of the features of his beloved; he fails, however, to improve her character as well and finds her a real menace to his future happiness when his old flame unexpectedly returns to him.

Lady in the Fog (*Scotland Yard Inspector*) (1952) featured Cesar Romero as an American reporter cracking a murder mystery. In an ingenious example of cost-cutting *and* providing the kind of off-beat location that was so valuable in camouflaging a commonplace plot, the climactic gunfight took place in a deserted film studio. **The Gambler and the Lady** (1952) starred Dane Clark as the gullible gambler who comes unstuck with a lady from high society as well as with some racketeers infesting London's gambling belt. Clark was lucky

in being called back to England for two further films under the Lippert-Exclusive arrangement; otherwise these visiting stars were usually changed for each picture, or did one further title at best.

Mantrap (*Man in Hiding*) and **Four-Sided Triangle** (both 1953) were outside the Lippert deal, being made as co-productions with Alexander Paal. The first had Paul Henreid as a lawyer clearing an escaped convict of murder while ninth in the cast Kay Kendall, as the hero's knowing secretary, gave a lively performance that walked away with the acting honours and earmarked her for better things. **Four-Sided Triangle** deserves special comment as Hammer's first venture into fantasy and science-fiction, although its idea of duplicating a woman to make up for the

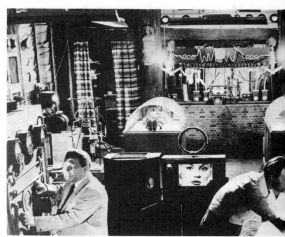

Four-Sided Triangle: James Hayter, Barbara Payton, Stephen Murray.

loss of the original had already been tried in *Stolen Face*. Here the scientific aspects were emphasised to such a degree that, as with many other science-fiction pictures, these became the main point of appeal and "name" stars could be largely dispensed with, allowing the money to be invested in sets and laboratory paraphernalia. Two scientists working in a barn in a remote village both fall in love with the same girl (Barbara Payton, the one player with a modest star reputation). She elects to marry one (John Van Eyssen), leaving the other (Stephen Murray) to overcome his grief by perfecting a machine to duplicate her exactly. Such is his success that his creation also prefers his romantic rival! Ultimately creator and creation perish in one of those fires that have proved such a handy way of clearing up the plot and making life on this planet safe from the errors of science — unless a sequel should be demanded . . .

Continuing with Lippert, Exclusive put Barbara Payton into **The Flanagan Boy** *(Bad Blonde)* (1953), directed by Hollywood's Reginald LeBorg and featuring Tony Wright as the boxer driven to suicide by his passion for Miss Payton's blonde features. Hammer came up with **Spaceways** (1953), the first British picture to cash in on the Hollywood space cycle that had included *Rocketship X-M* and *Destination Moon*. The space aspect provided an ingenious twist to a crime story with Howard Duff as the space scientist who is accused of having killed his wife and her lover and placed their bodies in an experimental satellite that will circle the earth until long after he is dead. To clear himself, the scientist goes up in a rocket to recover the satellite.

Face the Music *(The Black Glove)* (1954) mixed music and crime with Alex Nicol as an idolised trumpeter topping the bill at the London Palladium and escaping his fans long enough to solve a murder case; Kenny Baker's musical contributions helped widen the film's appeal. **Blood Orange** *(Three Stops to Murder)* was made for another American distributor besides Lippert and had Tom Conway playing himself as a detective solving a mystery against a background of London fashion.

Life With the Lyons (1954) saw Exclusive catering primarily for the home market with director Val Guest initiating a lasting if intermittent association with Exclusive and Hammer in his adaptation of the long-running radio series. This placed the Lyon family — Ben and Bebe, Richard and Barbara — plus other familiar characters in a new house with teething troubles that included an exploding kitchen and flooded basement. Results were encouraging enough for a sequel to be shortly forthcoming — **The Lyons in Paris** (1955) — with Ben and Bebe celebrating their silver anniversary in La Belle France.

The Lyons in Paris: Bebe, Ben, Richard and Barbara Lyo

The House Across the Lake *(Heat Wave)* was for Lippert and out of the ordinary in two ways. First, it was the only picture of these early years that went to a British distributor other than Exclusive. Second, it employed the writing and directing talents of Ken Hughes, who fashioned a very slick and effective imitation of Hollywood melodrama at its best in telling his story of an American pulp novelist (Alex Nicol) who becomes the "fall guy" in a woman's scheme to murder her wealthy husband (Sidney James). Otherwise, Hughes was busy turning out similar pictures for another British company, Anglo-Amalgamated, that like Hammer had become skilled in supplying thrillers for the American market.

Paulette Goddard came over for **The Stranger Came Home** *(The*

Unholy Four), partnering another American actor, William Sylvester (who had made his entire career in Britain), in a story of a financier who is a victim of amnesia and suspected of murder. **Five Days** *(Paid to Kill)* (1954) used a familiar but still ingenious plot idea of a bankrupt financier (Dane Clark) blackmailing a friend into killing him so that his wife can benefit from his life insurance, then having considerable difficulty in staying alive when he changes his mind. **36 Hours** *(Terror Street)* (1954) featured Dan Duryea as the man with limited time to solve his wife's murder. **Mask of Dust** *(A Race for Life)* (1954) starred Richard Conte and Mari Aldon against a motor racing backcloth with Stirling Moss as one of several guest performers. **Third Party Risk** *(Deadly Game)* (1955) had its source in a novel by Nicolas Bentley and a different background (Spain); its story of Lloyd Bridges caught up in a smuggling racket was very much in the style of Hammer's other pictures of this time. **Murder by Proxy** *(Blackout)* (1955) presented Dane Clark as a hard-up American taking money to marry a beautiful heiress (Belinda Lee) and finding himself caught up in murder. **The Glass Cage** *(The Glass Tomb)* (1955) was a London fairground mystery with John Ireland and a young Honor Blackman; it was also the last in the programme of films for Lippert, which soon after gave up distribution and affiliated with 20th Century-Fox for the production of Regalscope low-budget pictures in Hollywood.

Left over for a footnote to this period are Hammer's first two ventures into colour, a costly addition that probably paid off with **Men of Sherwood Forest** (1954), which also introduced Hammer to the field of costume adventure. Don Taylor was an economy equivalent of Errol Flynn as Robin Hood, and together with

Reginald Beckwith's Friar Tuck lent a helping hand to Patrick Holt's Richard the Lionheart. Less successful was the added expense of colour to **Break in the Circle** (1955), a lively drama with Forrest Tucker as the professional smuggler involved in helping a Polish scientist escape from the Communists and also thwarting the double-crossing intentions of his employer (Marius Goring). It was perhaps symptomatic of the declining need for this kind of picture that it should have waited two years for an American release and then have been stripped of its colour and 23 minutes of running time.

What had happened was that audiences were increasingly finding their everyday entertainment on TV. Cinema audiences had to be given more for their money: films had become longer (and, through Cinema-Scope, wider), eliminating most of the need for long supporting features. Fewer bookings were available as a result of cinema closures, and this reduced income since B features received fixed rentals regardless of the main feature's success.

For international success, a film now needed major stars (beyond the resources of a small company like Hammer) or some extraordinary aspect of appeal to compensate for their absence. Hammer found the latter element in making *The Quatermass Xperiment* and quickly left behind the minor but busy period covered in this chapter. Exclusive was soon to fade from the picture, releasing only a few minor Hammer productions (mostly featurettes), one or two independently made British B features, and some odd American titles, plus of course continuing to supply its older pictures for repertory bookings; it was finally liquidated in 1968. The rest of the story is Hammer's alone.

THE RETURN OF FRANKENSTEIN

Hammer's first venture into horror more properly belongs to the science fiction field that the company had already explored in *Four-Sided Triangle* and *Spaceways*; it also had the same kind of built-in acceptance as the Lyons' comedies, having been tested on the fireside audience in Britain, and it continued Hammer's formula of having an American actor as star to ease the film into the world market. This was **The Quatermass Xperiment** (1955), derived from Nigel Kneale's sensationally successful TV serial of July-August 1953, with the spelling of the word "Experiment" adjusted to emphasise the film's adults-only "X" certificate (in America the film was retitled *The Creeping Unknown* by United Artists).

Val Guest's direction and adaptation, with American writer Richard Landau, preserved much of the quality of the original, including the keen sense of British settings, although it didn't quite have the same feeling of urgency and spontaneity as the story had had on TV, nor the advantage of the nerve-stretching serial format. Brian Donlevy was dependable as Professor Quatermass, the man who has put Britain's first rocketship in space and investigates the disappearance of two of the spacemen on its return, together with the mysterious changes that have affected the only visible survivor. Richard Wordsworth gave a moving portrayal of the latter figure, slowly succumbing to the alien force that possesses him and transforms him into a monster which, in the tense climax, is electrocuted when it hides out in Westminster Abbey.

The Quatermass Xperiment: Richard Wordsworth.

The film had a successful West End run and then formed half of a memorable double-bill with the French thriller *Rififi* on the ABC circuit. Hammer's next science-fiction thriller **X — the Unknown** (1956), proved similarly useful for packaging with another French picture, *The Fiends*, to provide an impressive value double-"X" programme. With *X — the Unknown* (1956), one finds Hammer giving Jimmy Sangster his first big break, using his original screenplay. Sangster had joined Hammer back in the *Dick Barton* days, worked as the assistant director on such films as *Cloudburst*, and risen to be production manager, a function he retained on *X — the Unknown*. Since then, of course, he has become one of Hammer's principal creative talents, as writer, producer and director. Here his screenplay dealt with a monstrous sludge which quietly slithers out of the ground after an earth disturbance in a remote area of Scottish moorland and eats up members of the local population until an atomic scientist, Dr. Adam Royston (Hollywood's Dean Jagger), deduces that the thing is after radioactive material and works out a way to corner it at an atomic research station and put it out of action. Hammer's rising importance was reflected in attracting a distinguished Ealing Studios' director, Leslie Norman, to make the film, and selling it to a major Hollywood company, Warner Bros., for an American release.

A film version of Nigel Kneale's second Quatermass serial quickly followed in the same year; Brian Donlevy again played the Professor and Val Guest directed. This was **Quatermass II** *(Enemy from Space)* and again had alien forces taking over human beings, though this time more surreptitiously as part of a plan to infiltrate an industrial research plant and use its facilities to work out an

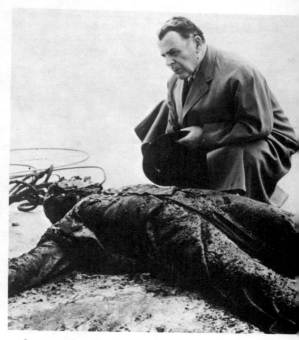

Quatermass II: Brian Donlevy.

adjustment to the earth's environment. A further Nigel Kneale TV work, a play called *The Creature*, provided the basis for **The Abominable Snowman** (1957) with Forrest Tucker as the botanist and Peter Cushing the scientist who led an expedition into the Himalayas to find the mysterious half-beast, half-human Yeti.

Before these last two films, however, Hammer had already made its big step of moving into period horror for **The Curse of Frankenstein** (1957), after the company's investigations had led to the conclusion that audiences preferred monsters closer to a sympathetic human form rather than completely "out of this world". Mary Shelley's famous story of Frankenstein and his monster seemed ideal, especially as it was in the public domain. Jimmy Sangster based his screenplay on this, rather than Universal's classic horror film of 1931. The plot was nevertheless much the same, with Peter Cushing as Baron

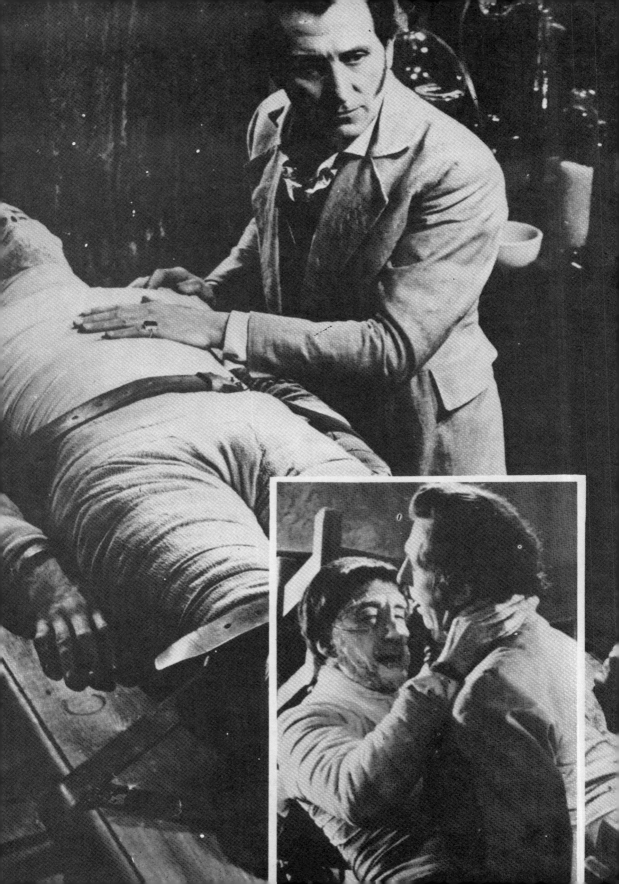

Victor Frankenstein who lets his scientific zeal get the better of him when he murders a great scientist in order to obtain his brain to put into the creature he is assembling from human parts. His associate, Paul Krempe (Robert Urquhart), is so horrified that he tries to stop Frankenstein; in their struggle the brain is damaged so that when the creature (played by a busy but then little-known actor, Christopher Lee) comes to life he possesses violent criminal tendencies which result in a series of murders for which Frankenstein is blamed and condemned to death at the guillotine.

The film's main drawback was that it was denied the use of the celebrated make-up that Universal's Jack Pierce had devised for Karloff's monster and Hammer's make-up man, Phil Leakey, was not quite able to match the impact of that masterful creation. But the film had several advantages: it had the novelty appeal of being a fully-fledged *British* horror picture; it was filmed in colour, then a fairly infrequent addition to this kind of film, but most effective in heightening the impact of bleeding parts and fiery violence; it took its subject seriously, helped by Peter Cushing's sensitive performance as the Baron, and restored dignity to a monster that, in Universal's hands, had degenerated into a stooge for Abbott and Costello; and, finally, it was made with care, if not perhaps inspiration, and its sets, music and photography were all excellent. When the film turned out to be a big success in England and the biggest dollar-earner that British studios had produced that year, Hammer were not slow to announce a sequel and seize the next obvious subject for re-make treatment, Dracula.

With the same leading players and virtually the same production team, **Dracula** (American title, *Horror of Dracula*) (1958) had equally spec-

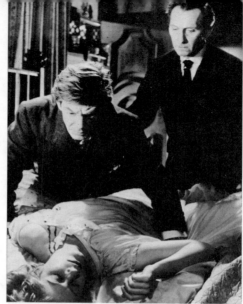

Dracula: Melissa Stribling, Michael Gough, Peter Cushing.

tacular box-office results. Christopher Lee emerged from monster make-up to chill audiences as the yellow-eyed Count Dracula, while Peter Cushing portrayed his perennial nemesis, the

Dracula: Valerie Gaunt, Christopher Lee.

eminent vampirologist, Dr. Van Helsing, armed with crucifixes, garlic flowers and the other paraphernalia of his rather specialised trade. Again in colour, the film was far more explicit than the original Bela Lugosi version, with Dracula's victims actually enjoying rather than resisting his neck-biting advances. The film's most memorable moments included the scene in which Dracula's librarian (John Van Eyssen) drives a stake into

Dracula: Christopher Lee, John Van Eyssen.

the heart of a beautiful woman resting in a coffin, turning her into an aged hag before our eyes; and . the showdown between Dracula and Van Helsing in the former's castle, the Count being trapped in a shaft of bright sunlight and withering away into a handful of dust, a signet ring, and a hank of hair that is blown across the floor by a draught in the air.

The Revenge of Frankenstein

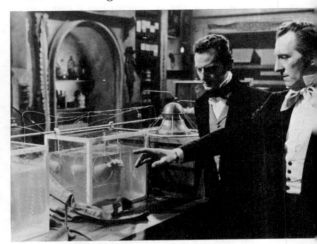

The Revenge of Frankenstein: Francis Matthews, Peter Cushing.

(1958) saved Peter Cushing's neck from the guillotine poised to sever it at the end of the previous Frankenstein film — a handy priest had taken his place at the beheading — and allowed the Baron to masquerade as a Dr. Stein, continuing his experiments and this time creating a monster (Michael Gwynn) with a brain that is normal until it is damaged in a scrap — whereupon the creature turns into a crazed figure with an appetite for human flesh. Dr. Stein barely escapes an enraged mob and takes up residence on London's Harley Street as a Professor Frank.

By now the Hollywood studios were only too happy to admit that Hammer had the knack for turning out polished but economically budgeted horror pictures and began handing over properties they owned

The Mummy: Christopher Lee, Peter Cushing.

for the re-make treatment. For Universal, Jimmy Sangster made a new treatment of the old 1932 screenplay of **The Mummy** (1959), with Christopher Lee taking on the title role, his mummy being the former lover of an entombed princess who comes to life to avenge the desecration of her tomb by a group of explorers. Only the likeness of a modern woman (Yvonne Furneaux) to his love of old distracts him from his mission and he carries her off through a swamp, there to be shot down by a posse of Englishmen. Peter Cushing portrayed a lucky survivor of the Egyptian expedition that had found the tomb.

The Mummy: Yvonne Furneaux, Christopher Lee.

Jimmy Sangster also revised the Barré Lyndon play that Paramount had filmed as *The Man in Half-Moon Street* (1945); this new version, called **The Man Who Could Cheat Death** (1959), starred Anton Diffring as the 104-year-old who keeps himself

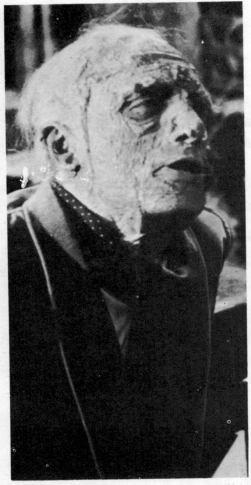

The Man Who Could Cheat Death: Anton Diffring.

looking only a third of his real age by a periodic gland operation. When his regular surgeon declines to renew the treatment, the man kills him and kidnaps a woman (Hazel Court), blackmailing her surgeon lover (Christopher Lee) into operating on him. However, he is double-crossed and lapses into his real age like Oscar Wilde's Dorian Gray, quickly perishing in a dramatically contrived fire.

The Stranglers of Bombay (1960) is set in India in 1826 and deals with the cult of thugee or thuggism which broke out when worshippers of the goddess Kali began robbing, strangling and often mutilating thousands of victims, interring them in mass graves and undermining the authority of the British East India Company. Eventually the secret organisation in the film is broken up but the subject gave scope for such horrific moments as blindings, evisceration, and the tossing about of human heads. Mercifully, and perhaps respecting the more realistic basis of this film, Hammer shot it in monochrome, dispensing with the opportunity to sensationalise in colour.

Stranglers of Bombay: George Pastell.

Stranglers of Bombay: Marie Devereux, Guy Rolfe.

The Two Faces of Dr. Jekyll: Paul Massie, Christopher Lee.

The Two Faces of Dr. Jekyll *(House of Fright)* (1960) was Hammer's first serious treatment of the Robert Louis Stevenson novel after the comic use made of the Jekyll and Hyde idea in *The Ugly Duckling* (see next chapter). Writer Wolf Mankowitz gave the familiar story a new and ingenious twist, making Hyde a clean-shaven, debonair, coolly sadistic figure, rather than the hairy monster of earlier film treatments. In contrast, Dr. Jekyll was the bearded, sombre scientist who changes his personality out of scientific curiosity, discovers in it a useful method of avenging his wife's infidelity, and, having killed both her and her lover, finds himself unable to resist further murders. Paul Massie played the dual role.

The Brides of Dracula (1960) retained Peter Cushing as Van Helsing but substituted David Peel as the chief vampire in place of Christopher Lee. Peel's Baron Meinster is kept locked up in his castle by his mother (Martita Hunt) who procures female victims to satisfy his vampire urges, while Freda Jackson portrays his crazed and evil nurse who coaxes the dead victims back to life from their graves in the middle of the night. Meinster eventually burns to death in an old windmill whose shadow casts a cruciform shape on the ground. The unusually well-etched female characterisations and general mood of the film have made this one of the most highly admired Hammer horror films among connoisseurs of the genre.

The Brides of Dracula: David Peel.

The Brides of Dracula: Martita Hunt, Yvonne Monlaur, Freda Jackson.

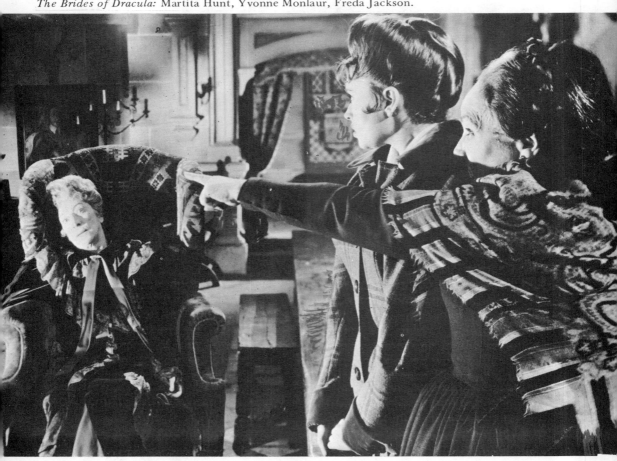

The Curse of the Werewolf (1961) took Hammer into another staple area of horror: lycanthropy. The film is a case-book study of a werewolf from birth — as the son of a deaf-mute servant girl raped by a fanged, unkempt beggar — to death from a silver bullet forged from a crucifix and fired by his compassionate stepfather at the top of a church tower. In between, young Leon gives away such clues to his unfortunate nature as causing the holy water in the font at his christening to boil over, leaving a trail of savaged animals in his childhood path, and (played by Oliver Reed as an adult) turning wolfman at

The Curse of the Werewolf: Oliver Reed.

the full moon to kill several people. A romantic attachment enables Leon to suppress his lycanthropic feelings until it is broken off, leading to the tragic conclusion.

The Terror of the Tongs (1961) was a follow-up to *The Stranglers of Bombay*, exchanging the thugee cult of India for Hong Kong's Red Dragon Tong of the 1910 period — a ruthless secret society engaged in white slavery and opium smuggling. The film's hero (Geoffrey Toone), out to avenge his daughter's death, brings about the downfall of the society's leader, Chung King (Christopher Lee), but not before he has been subjected to such refined tortures as bone-scraping.

The Terror of the Tongs.

The Curse of the Werewolf: Catherine Feller, Oliver Reed.

The Phantom of the Opera: Edward de Souza, Herbert Lom, Heather Sears.

This was the first of Hammer's period horror films to be assigned to a director other than Terence Fisher, though the capable Fisher was soon back with Hammer's re-make of **The Phantom of the Opera** (1962), giving Herbert Lom the role that Lon Chaney and Claude Rains had taken in earlier versions. Compared to Hollywood's efforts, Roy Ashton's make-up of the Phantom rather disappointed, but the sets — especially the underground lair of the title character — lent an impressive atmosphere to the film. Heather Sears played the beautiful young opera singer who is given her big chance by the Phantom and is saved from accidental death by the sacrifice of his own life.

Captain Clegg.

Captain Clegg *(Night Creatures)* (1962) was a somewhat more horrific pirate adventure than those discussed in the next chapter, about smuggling

38

in the Romney Marshes by the celebrated pirate Captain Clegg and his men, the "Marsh Phantoms". They are capable of frightening an observer to death, disguising a look-out as a scarecrow, conveying contraband alcohol in hearses, and otherwise lending a grotesque note to rural normality. Peter Cushing portrayed the apparently benign village vicar, Doctor Blyss, alias Captain Clegg.

In **The Damned** *(These Are the Damned)* (1963), Hammer had a problem film that took some time to come down off the shelf. Director Joseph Losey and writer Evan Jones had fashioned an intellectually chilling story of a group of children reared in an artificial, radioactive world to enable them to survive in the aftermath of an atomic war, and worked in another aspect of a sick society in the motor-bike gang led by Oliver Reed. Cut even before its British release, then sheared more drastically for its eventual American appearance *The Damned* was paired off with Hammer's equally unsuccessful adult thriller *Maniac*.

The company got back into its stride with **Kiss of the Vampire** (1964), intelligently directed by Don Sharp and substituting Noel Willman's Doctor Ravna and Clifford Evans' Professor Zimmer for Dracula and Van Helsing in a story of a honey-

mooning couple stranded in a Bavarian forest and foolishly accepting the hospitality of Ravna, whose castle is the headquarters of the local vampire circle. The young wife (Jennifer Daniel) is rescued by Zimmer's intervention, which leads to a swarm of avenging bats destroying the vampires who include such decorative players among their number as Isobel Black.

In **The Evil of Frankenstein** (1964), Baron Frankenstein (Peter Cushing) is on the run from another band of outraged villagers, when he comes across one of his earlier creations, a semi-human monster that has been preserved in a glacier. Recruiting a mesmerist to help reactivate its damaged brain, the rest of the creature responding to a charge of electricity, the Baron soon finds himself competing for control of the thing which is sent by the hynoptist on some errands of theft and murder. Even when Frankenstein retrieves his

The Evil of Frankenstein: Peter Cushing, Kiwi Kingston.

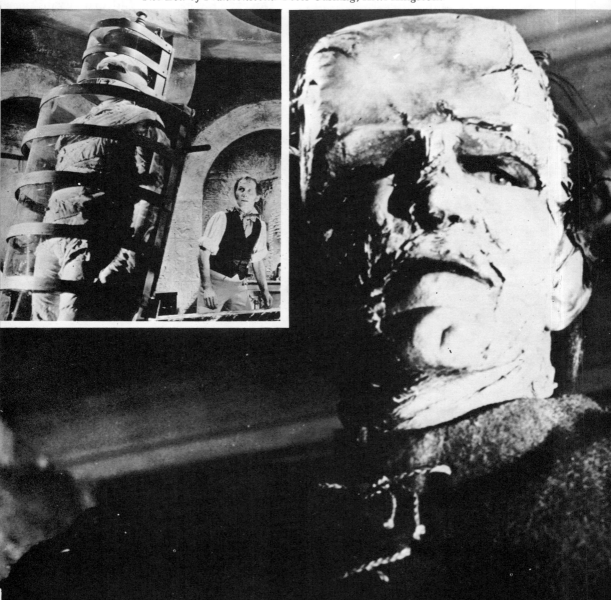

creation, he is unable to stop it getting drunk on brandy and then consuming an agonising dose of chloroform; both the Baron and the creature seemingly perish in a fire.

The Curse of the Mummy's Tomb and **The Gorgon** provided one of those neat double bills for British circuit release which Hammer were

The Gorgon.

The Curse of the Mummy's Tomb.

tending to prefer to the big single feature. This 1964 combination offered another Mummy (Dickie Owen) recklessly removed from the tombs of Egypt and taken on a world tour by an American showman, eventually awakening to wreak vengeance on those who have treated him so shabbily and then meeting his end in an underground sewer — plus a

return trip to Transylvania, where the villagers are being literally petrified by a female monster from a Greek fable, the Gorgon, with hissing serpents in her head of hair. The Gorgon turns out to have possessed the beautiful Carla (Barbara Shelley) and to be in cahoots with Peter Cushing's brain surgeon, Namaroff, leaving Christopher Lee as the university professor, Meister, to lead the forces of good to eventual victory.

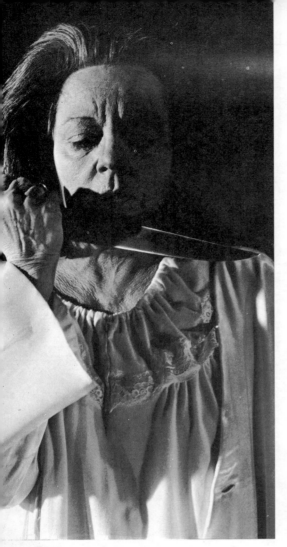

If Miss Bankhead had been chewing up the scenery in what seemed an imitation of Bette Davis's grotesque performance in *What Ever Happened to Baby Jane?*, Miss Davis herself, when she came to work for Hammer, contributed a performance that was a model of quiet discipline and finely effective detail in **The Nanny** (1965), a Jimmy Sangster script persuasively directed by Seth Holt and featuring the actress in the title role. The nanny's mind has almost been unhinged by the past tragedies in her life. She just fails to kill her young charge (William Dix), after watching an aunt (Jill Bennett) expire from a heart attack brought on by the discovery of the Nanny's disturbed mind. Her mental disturbance has been so skilfully disguised by her sweet nature that the boy's earlier accusations of her unfitness to look after him have naturally been disbelieved.

The Nanny: Bette Davis.

Fanatic: Tallulah Bankhead.

Fanatic (*Die! Die! My Darling*) (1965) was rather more ambitious — bringing Tallulah Bankhead back to the screen, obviously enjoying herself immensely as the mad Mrs. Trefoile, owner of a rambling country house who considers her dead son's fiancée to be betraying him by her plans to marry someone else. As the young woman who becomes Mrs. Trefoile's prisoner, and almost dies as a sacrifice to her dead son, Stefanie Powers gave a suitably distraught performance. Silvio Narizzano's stylish direction and Arthur Ibbetson's lush colour photography made the most of the literate script by Richard Matheson.

slitting the corpse's stomach open so that blood pours over the Count's remains, restoring him to his old form. The Count's new adventures in blood-sucking are ultimately brought to a halt again when he is cornered on frozen ice and skilful marksmanship causes it to break up around his feet and submerge the Count in running water which has a destructive effect on him. Appearing at the same time, **Plague of the Zombies**, was directed by a recent recruit to Hammer's directorial ranks, John Gilling, and concerned a voodoo cult in darkest Cornwall, with empty graves, the dead walking the countryside, the local squire (John Carson) creating a band of zombies to work an old tin-mine,

Plague of the Zombies: John Carson.

Dracula — Prince of Darkness: Andrew Keir, Suzan Farmer, Francis Matthews, Christopher Lee.

Dracula — Prince of Darkness (1966) began by repeating the ending of the original Hammer *Dracula* with the Count being reduced to a pile of ashes. It is not long, however, before one of the Count's faithful assistants has captured an unwary overnight visitor to Castle Dracula and suspended his dead body over the ashes,

Plague of the Zombies.

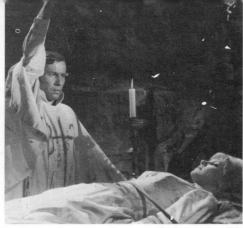

and the film's heroine (Diane Clare) being rescued in a fiery climax from the role of human sacrifice in a voodoo ceremony. Most impressive are the images of the dead rising from the ground, their fingers clawing away the earth in a green-hued graveyard.

John Gilling's **The Reptile** (1966) was also based on Cornwall (enabling further use of the sets provided for *Plague of the Zombies*). Here a village is in the grip of fear after a rash of deaths which are found to have been caused by snakebite, a phenomenon ultimately explained as resulting from the periodic transformation of Anna Franklyn (Jacqueline Pearce) into a

The Reptile: Jacqueline Pearce, Jennifer Daniel.
The Reptile: Jennifer Daniel, Ray Barrett.

snakewoman as the result of a curse placed on her by an obscure Malayan sect. This unhappy figure, a victim of circumstances beyond her control, is ultimately consumed by flames. *The Reptile* was paired off in British

The Reptile: Jacqueline Pearce.

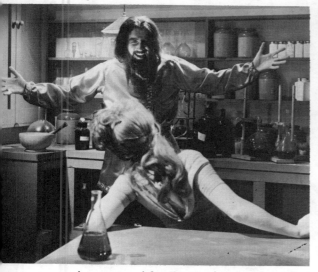

Rasputin — the Mad Monk: Christopher Lee.

Rasputin — the Mad Monk: Christopher Lee, Barbara Shelley.

cinemas with **Rasputin — the Mad Monk,** starring Christopher Lee under Don Sharp's direction. The film shows Rasputin leaving the religious order to exploit his strange powers of healing, hypnotising the Tsarina's lady-in-waiting into injuring the Tsar's young son so that he can effect a cure and worm his way into power at the court. Though budgetary restrictions inevitably told against a lavish depiction of Tsarist Russia, the film was otherwise effective Hammer horror, with a dismembered hand and an acid-scarred face to please the regular audience and a final spectacular deathfall by Rasputin over a parapet, to round things off.

The Old Dark House (1966) was a rare instance of Hammer ceding creative authority to another film-maker — William Castle, then a skilful practitioner in exploitation "quickies". However, despite the presence of such entertaining artists as Joyce Grenfell, Robert Morley and Fenella Fielding, this re-make of James Whale's classic of 1932 was such a misfire blend of comedy and shock that it only escaped into a quiet second-feature niche in Britain four years after it was made (although American audiences saw it much earlier in 1963).

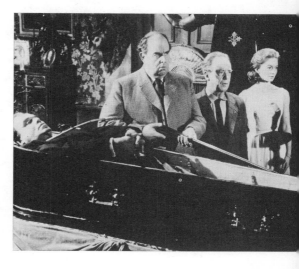

The Old Dark House: Peter Bull, Robert Morley, Mervyn Johns, Janette Scott.

Nigel Kneale returned to Hammer's "script crypt" to write the screenplay of **The Witches** (*The Devil's Own*) (1966), all about a woman (Joan Fontaine) who returns to the tranquil, cosy English countryside after an alarming experience with voodoo in Africa, only to find herself involved in a local witch-cult presided over by Stephanie Bax (Kay Walsh). She is barely in time to save a virgin schoolgirl (Ingrid Brett) from being sacrificed to ensure Stephanie's immortality during an orgy in a ruined church attended by the locals as a lively alternative to parish bingo.

Frankenstein Created Woman and **The Mummy's Shroud**, the last film made by Hammer at Bray Studios, formed Hammer's contribution to summer filmgoing in 1967 in another double-"X" double-bill. In the first, Peter Cushing laid out on a slab as the frozen corpse of Baron Frankenstein, is electrically restored to life by faithful friends. This time he not only revives the drowned body of a young girl (Susan Denberg) but also transfers

The Mummy's Shroud: Maggie Kimberley.

to her the soul of her boyfriend, guillotined for a murder he hasn't committed, so that she can be the instrument of his revenge before killing herself a second time. The second half of the programme offered yet another Mummy (Eddie Powell), which is again removed against local advice from his Egyptian resting place and taken to a museum. Stirred to life, he kills those who have disturbed him, until the archaeologist Claire (Maggie Kimberley) finds the sacred words that can crumble him to dust.

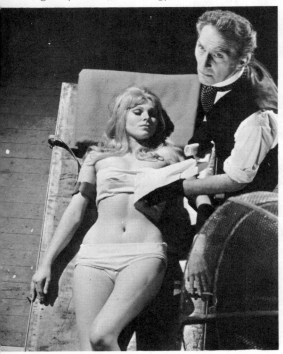

Frankenstein Created Woman:
Susan Denberg, Peter Cushing.

The Mummy's Shroud: Catherine Lacey.

The proceedings are enlivened considerably by Catherine Lacey's performance as an old fortune-teller, toothless, foaming at the lips, and gazing very clearly into her crystal ball.

It was now time for Hammer to embark on the filming of the last Quatermass TV serial, **Quatermass and the Pit** *(Five Million Years to Earth)* (1967), with director Roy Ward Baker resuming his career with the first of several films for Hammer. The story deals with the discovery of a large buried object during some excavations in London. It is found to contain the remains of alien creatures who attempted to conquer the Earth in prehistoric times. Though dead for so long, their residual power conjures up a frightening Devil that is only dispersed by toppling a large overhead crane on to its form. Andrew Keir took on the Quatermass role, James Donald portrayed a fellow scientist who sacrifices his life to make the Earth safe again for mankind, and there are some terrifying moments showing men possessed by the demonic power. Overall, however, the film was rather too thoughtful and sparing in its horror ingredients to entirely satisfy those with firm expectations based on the film being a Hammer production.

Miss Bette Davis returned to Hammer to make **The Anniversary**

Quatermass and the Pit.

The Anniversary: Bette Davis.

(1968), an unusual venture in comic Grand Guignol, with a Jimmy Sangster script and Roy Ward Baker direction. Here the actress throws discretion to the winds as Mrs. Taggart, the widow and mother who has never really severed the umbilical cord between her and the three sons she dominates at annual reunions, resorting to the most unscrupulous methods to achieve her ends. One-eyed, exotically-gowned, Mrs. Taggart is a memorable tyrant.

The work of popular novelist Dennis Wheatley seemed to suddenly engage Hammer's attention; they released two films from his work in successive weeks of 1968. First was **The Devil Rides Out** *(The Devil's Bride)* with Christopher Lee as the Duc de Richleau pitting his knowledge of devil worship against the band of Satanists led by Charles Gray as the

The Lost Continent: Suzanna Leigh.

The Lost Continent: James Cossins (right).

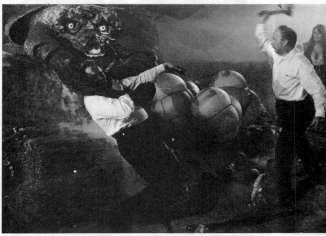

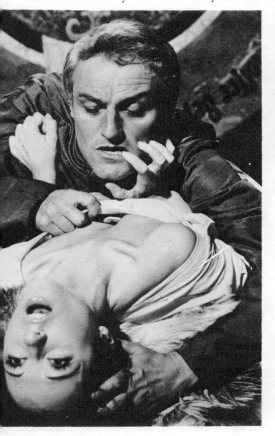

high priest Mocata. **The Lost Continent**, produced and directed by Michael Carreras, concerned a group of misfit passengers on a limping old tramp steamer in uncharted seas who discover a lost world of outsize octopuses, giant crustaceans, and a strange race of ancient castaways, led by an evil boy king, who use gas-filled balloons to travel across areas of carnivorous seaweed. An unwieldy combination of personal dramas, science-fiction and period maritime adventure, the film has sufficient zest in its approach to the more outlandish dangers of its story to pitch it into the horror category.

The Devil Rides Out: Charles Gray, Nike Arrighi.

For Hammer's fourth Dracula story, **Dracula Has Risen from the Grave** (1968), Freddie Francis took over the direction from Terence Fisher and hinted at his past as a brilliant cinematographer by some interesting filter effects to greet Dracula's appearances. As in *Dracula — Prince of Darkness*, Van Helsing is not recruited to fight Dracula and instead the Church, represented by Rupert Davies' Monsignor, takes on the task. The sexuality involved in vampirism is made even more explicit, as Dracula's advances are eagerly received by his victims. He is revived from an icy grave by the blood of a wounded priest whom he recruits as a slave; but he is later forced to retreat from the crucifix brandished at him by the Monsignor, loses the services of the cleric, and ends up impaled on an enormous cross.

Dracula Has Risen from the Grave: Christopher Lee, Veronica Carlson.

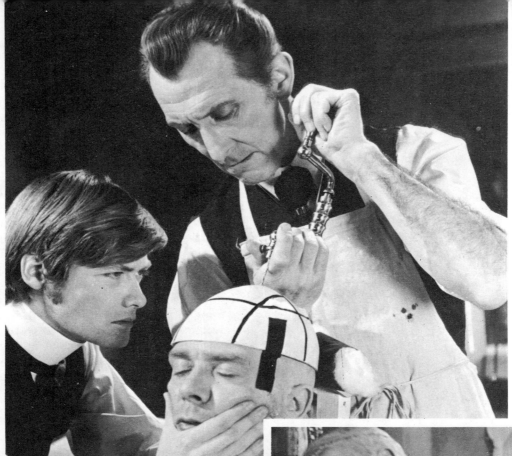

"Frankenstein! I thought the world had heard the last of you!" exclaims an unimaginative soul when Frankenstein rises again in **Frankenstein Must Be Destroyed** (1969). Just as Jimmy Sangster obtained a writing break from Hammer with *X — the Unknown*, so here Hammer's regular assistant director, Bert Batt, was encouraged to provide a script from a story he devised with Anthony Nelson Keys, one of Hammer's key production personnel. The cast, too, besides the familiar face of Peter Cushing as the Baron, had an actor called Simon Ward, since made famous by *Young Winston*, demonstrating Hammer's continual interest in developing new talent. This time the Baron tries his hand at brain transplanting and kidnaps an insane surgeon who has the know-how to help him but who dies before being of

Frankenstein Must Be Destroyed: Peter Cushing, Simon Ward, Freddie Jones, Veronica Carlson.

Frankenstein Must Be Destroyed.

The Vampire Lovers (1970) was Hammer's first and (to date) only co-production with Hollywood's leading horror specialists American International, who have been responsible for most of the Edgar Allan Poe pictures. This film tapped a new source of classic horror literature, the

The Vampire Lovers: Madeleine Smith, Ingrid Pitt.

The Vampire Lovers: Pippa Steele.

use, except to provide his brain for the Baron to place in the body of a dead professor. The latter recovers, now believing himself to be the surgeon, and goes to visit his wife who naturally doesn't recognise him and is terrified by his scarred features. Freddie Jones plays the confused unfortunate who seeks revenge on Frankenstein by luring him into a house and setting it on fire. This complicated plot was more than usually interesting and Terence Fisher's direction gave it lively treatment.

New directorial blood was interestingly in evidence when TV director Peter Sasdy directed **Taste the Blood of Dracula** (1970). This time the story is set in Victorian times; three businessmen and a depraved aristocrat (Ralph Bates) acquire a phial containing the dried blood of the dead Dracula and retire to an old chapel to attempt to bring the Count back to life by a special formula. Once reactivated, Dracula (Christopher Lee) sets out on a mission of personal revenge until cornered in a chapel and apparently destroyed by the film's young hero (Anthony Corland).

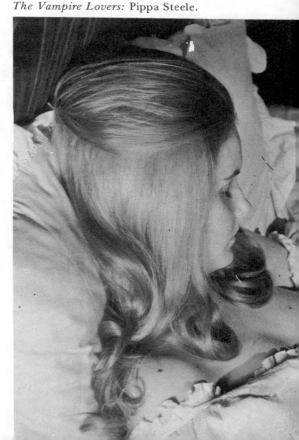

The Vampire Lovers: Ingrid Pitt, Kate O'Mara, Peter Cushing.

work of J. Sheridan Le Fanu, and injected an audacious dose of sex into the proceedings with Ingrid Pitt playing a beautiful female vampire, Mircalla Karnstein. Mircalla rises from the grave to avenge the deaths of her relatives, claiming not only the odd male as victim, but also several young girls, a lesbian aspect emphasised by her fanged attention to their breasts. Douglas Wilmer's Baron Hartog is Mircalla's chief adversary, arranging for a stake to penetrate her heart, while Peter Cushing's General Spielsdorf, father of one of her victims, makes doubly sure by removing her head!

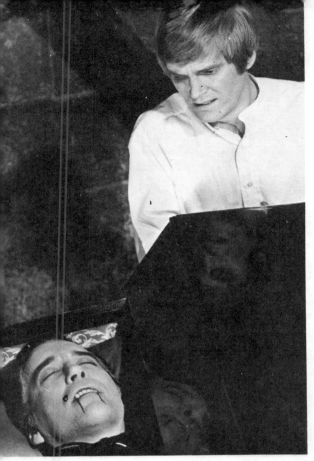

Dracula and Frankenstein were put in harness for a winter double-bill in 1970. **The Scars of Dracula** opens with yet another attempt by the long-suffering villagers to burn Christopher Lee's Count Dracula alive, after the death of a local girl. He survives, however, to become the coldly polite host to some intrepid visitors, flogging his crippled servant Klove (Patrick Troughton) when the latter helps some of them to escape. Simon (Dennis Waterman) is the bold avenger of a dead brother. Nevertheless he quails before Dracula's powers and is only saved from death by a bolt of lightning that plunges the Count's body, burning brightly, from the

The Scars of Dracula: Christopher Lee, Christopher Matthews.

The Scars of Dracula: Christopher Lee, Patrick Troughton.

The Scars of Dracula: Anoushka Hempel, Christopher Matthews.

Horror of Frankenstein: David Prowse.

Horror of Frankenstein: David Prowse, Joan Rice.

turret of his cliff-top castle. **Horror of Frankenstein**, one of Jimmy Sangster's pictures, presented Ralph Bates as Victor Frankenstein, a descendant of the original Baron, who follows in his father's footsteps, first reviving a dead tortoise, then hiring a grave robber (Dennis Price) to bring him some human parts, including the brain of a professor friend he poisons. The brain is accidentally dropped; it is no wonder then, that the monster (David Prowse), when brought to life during an electrical storm, is somewhat deranged and makes off to commit murder before its creator is able to lock it up in the cellar. The monster comes in useful for killing the dead grave-robber's wife (Joan Rice), and also Victor's housemaid-mistress (Kate O'Mara) when she threatens blackmail, but eventually perishes by accident in an acid bath. The plot essentially recapitulated the first *Frankenstein* film but was embroidered with some macabre touches of sick humour, with the monster being an unsympathetic thug, compared to the creature of latent sensitivity portrayed by Karloff in the real original of the series.

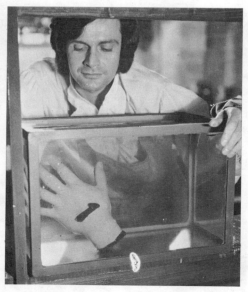

Horror of Frankenstein: Ralph Bates.

Horror of Frankenstein: David Prowse, Kate O'Mara.

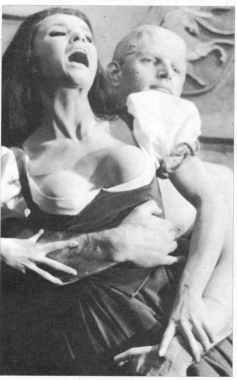

Jimmy Sangster's **Lust for a Vampire** (1971) followed on from *The Vampire Lovers* with Yutte Stensgaard portraying Mircalla and Michael Johnston playing the young student of the supernatural who comes to investigate the Karnstein legend, then falls in love with Mircalla and barely escapes with his life. From her opening revival when the blood from the slit throat of a peasant girl drips into her coffin and reconstitutes her, Yutte Stensgaard's Mircalla is a splendidly evil and ruthless figure, sinking her fangs into the throat of one of her teachers (Ralph Bates) at a girls' finishing school, as well as attacking the throat and breasts of a fellow pupil (Pippa Steel), and standing unscathed in the flames of a burning castle until a falling beam stakes her to death.

Above: *Lust for a Vampire:* Yutte Stensgaard. Left: *Lust for a Vampire:* Michael Johnson, Yutte Stensgaard.
Right: *Lust for a Vampire:* Yutte Stensgaard, Pippa Steele.

Countess Dracula: Ingrid Pitt.

Countess Dracula (1971) was not the addition to the regular series that its title would suggest but the story of an ageing Countess (Ingrid Pitt) who discovers by chance that the blood of young girls has a rejuvenating effect on her hard and wrinkled features. She commits murder to regain her youth fully and is forced to repeat the act to keep her good looks which enable her to romance a young Hussar (Sandor Eles) and even reach the altar with him before the game is given away when, as she speaks the marriage vows, her face crumples into hideous old age.

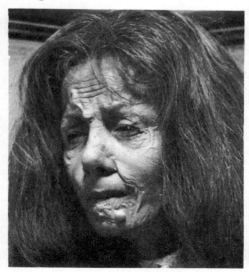

Hands of the Ripper: Eric Porter, Angharad Rees.

Late in 1971 **Hands of the Ripper** and **Twins of Evil** appeared in tandem. In the first, Eric Porter played the psychiatrist who employs Freudian techniques to try and cure the homicidal impulses that overtake Anna (Angharad Rees), the daughter of Jack the Ripper, every time she is kissed. ‑Several murders follow, including that of maid Dolly (Marjie Lawrence), a phoney medium (Dora Bryan) speared to a door, and a prostitute stabbed in the eye by a handful of hatpins. Even her benefactor almost loses hope when he is stabbed in the side, pursuing her to the whispering gallery at St. Paul's and coaxing her into a deathfall on top of

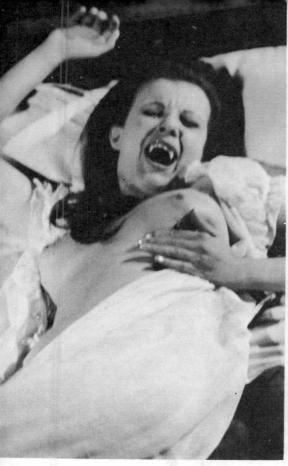

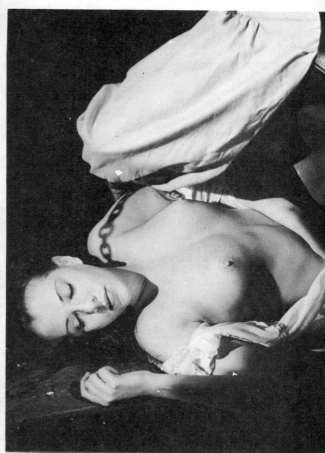

Twins of Evil: Madeleine Collinson.

Twins of Evil: Mary Collinson.

him. **Twins of Evil** brought us more of Mircalla Karnstein (Katya Keith), restored to life in the family castle during some sacrificial rites staged by a later member of her family (Damien Thomas), initiating him into the delights of vampirism, and setting off a whole rash of neck bitings. Peter Cushing leads the opposition as Gustav Weil, head of a witch-hunting group of Puritans called the Brotherhood. Weil beheads one of his two identical nieces (Madeleine Collinson) after she has become a vampire and her innocent sister (Mary Collinson) has almost been burned at the stake in an error of identification. The grim witch-hunter himself succumbs to an axe in the back. An unusually strong script, developing violent opposition between hunters and hunted, made this a more than usually impressive addition to the Hammer output.

Twins of Evil: Judy Matheson.

Blood from the Mummy's Tomb: James Villiers.

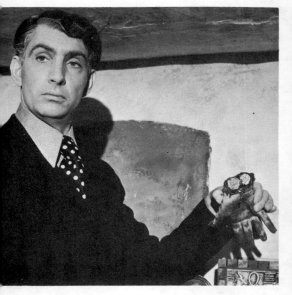

Blood from the Mummy's Tomb (1971) was based on a lesser known work by *Dracula's* author, Bram Stoker, and — like its predecessors in the Mummy field — is about an expedition to pillage the tombs of ancient Egypt, this time that of a queen whose severed hand still bleeds with a priceless ruby on one of its fingers. Her mummified body, the hand and other objects are brought back to England, where the ruby is given to Margaret (Valerie Leon), its transfer enabling the Egyptian queen to avenge the desecration of her tomb through its new owner. In Britain, the film was released in support of **Dr. Jekyll and Sister Hyde,** an intriguing variation on the usual story with Henry Jekyll (Ralph Bates) turning himself into a seductive female — the parts requiring, for the first time, two different players for the roles rather than one actor performing miracles of make-up and special effects. The transformation scenes were still quite a challenge, and the film had Sister Hyde (Martine Beswick) killing a series of women to further Jekyll's experiments in seeking the "elixir of life".

Blood from the Mummy's Tomb: Valerie Leon.

Dr. Jekyll and Sister Hyde: Ralph Bates, Martine Beswick.

Vampire Circus: Robert Tayman.

In **Vampire Circus** (1972), the setting is Serbia in the early nineteenth century, with a plague-ridden village visited by — as if it didn't have troubles enough! — a circus of vampires with the ability to change into animals. The film gave Robert Young his first chance to direct a feature, and Hammer's faith was repaid with a precise and effective piece of film-making.

Demons of the Mind (1972), given less than the usual widespread release of a Hammer picture, recalled the first attempts of psychiatry to control the human mind. Robert Hardy plays the part of a Baron in the Bavaria of the 1830s who believes that his family is doomed by hereditary evil and who keeps his son (Shane Briant) and daughter (Gillian Hills) locked away,

Demons of the Mind: Yvonne Mitchell, Gillian Hills.

Vampire Circus: Elizabeth Seal, Adrienne Corri, Anthony Corlan.

Demons of the Mind: Yvonne Mitchell, Robert Hardy, Patrick Magee.

mistakenly believing them to be insane. Patrick Magee appears as the doctor who discovers that the Baron has in fact been subconsciously willing his son to commit a series of murders. In the final showdown with the angered villagers the Baron is staked through the stomach by a burning cross; only his daughter escapes to a new life.

Dracula A.D.1972: Christopher Lee.

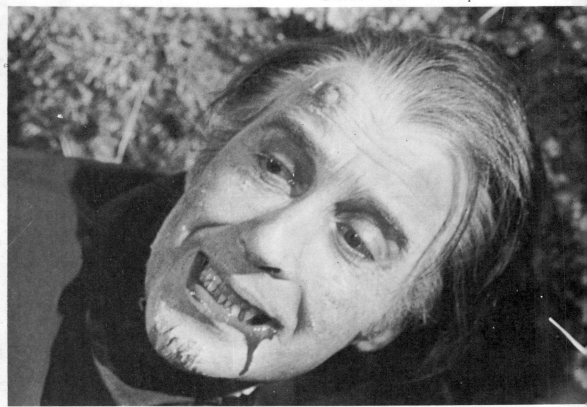

Dracula A.D. 1972 (1972) boldly attempted to weld the old and the new, with a disciple of Dracula (Christopher Neame) called Alucard (Dracula spelled backwards) organising a black magic ceremony in a Chelsea churchyard with some sensation-seeking teenagers. Soon Dracula's shrivelled remains become the man himself (Christopher Lee) and no one's neck is safe in the area. Fortunately, Peter Cushing is at hand in the customary form of Van Helsing to prevent Dracula taking his revenge on young Jessica Van Helsing (Stephanie Beacham) and the final showdown between the two long-standing enemies proves to be splendid stuff.

Dracula A.D. 1972: Caroline Munro, Christopher Lee.

The Satanic Rites of Dracula: Peter Cushing.

In the latest addition to the Dracula subsection of Hammer activity, called **The Satanic Rites of Dracula** (1973), the police and British security forces call in Van Helsing (Peter Cushing) to help them investigate a Black Mass which has been held at a large country house, with a top government minister as one of the participants. The house is guarded by youths dressed in storm-trooper black and vampire girls are found to be lying in coffins in the dank cellars. Soon Van Helsing discovers that his old adversary Dracula (Christopher Lee once more) is behind it all and has his niece Jessica (this time played by Joanna Lumley) lined up for a special role on the sacrificial altar. That Dracula is reduced to a pile of dust at the end will prove no surprise.

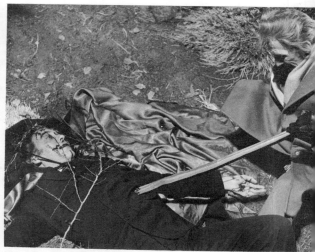

The Satanic Rites of Dracula: Christopher Lee, Peter Cushing.

Frankenstein and the Monster from Hell: David Prowse, Peter Cushing, Shane Briant.

Peter Cushing's Frankenstein also lived on in **Frankenstein . . . and the Monster from Hell** (1973) as Dr. Victor, the doctor at an asylum at Carlsbad. He is recognised by one of his most fervent admirers, Dr. Helder (Shane Briant), whose imitative experiments have earned him a place in the institution. Soon the newcomer discovers that Frankenstein is completing a monster from parts of the inmates who have died. Eventually the monster escapes and is forced into a fight with a throng of raving lunatics.

Kronos: Wanda Ventham.

Also from Hammer in 1973 came **Kronos**, the story of an early nineteenth century vampire hunter, Captain Kronos (Horst Janson), who with Professor Grost (John Cater), investigates an outbreak of vampirism before riding off into the sunset for other adventures.

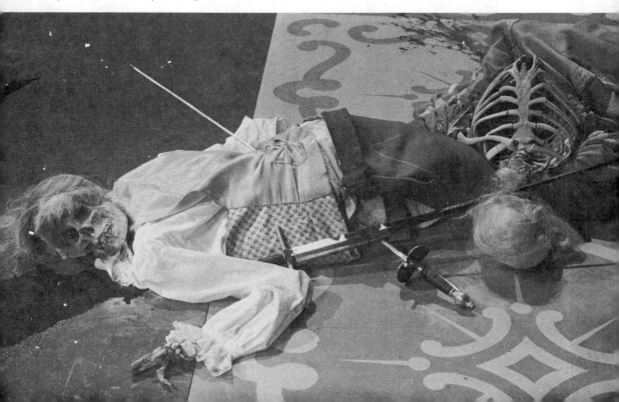

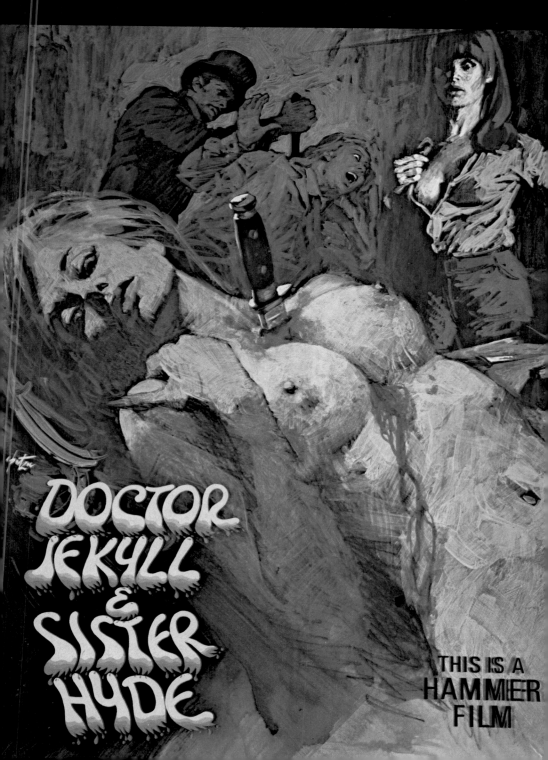

DOCTOR JEKYLL & SISTER HYDE

THIS IS A HAMMER FILM

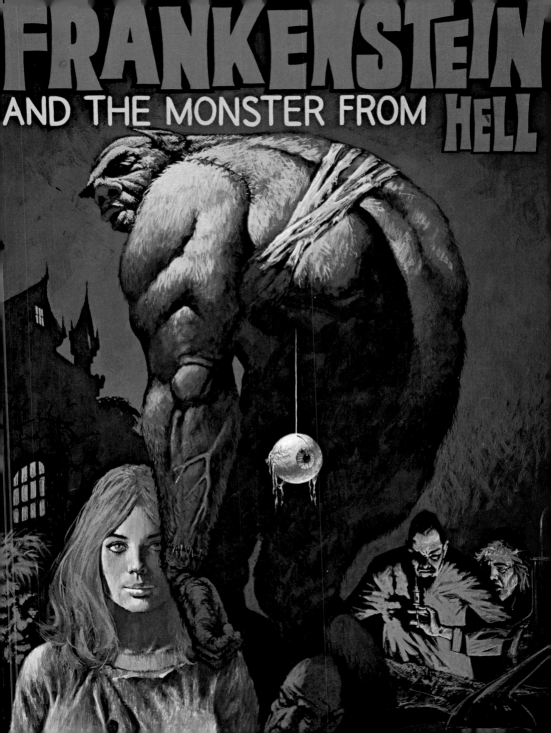

Victim of his Imagination

HAMMER'S OTHER WORLDS

Hammer's first big successes in horror, beginning with *The Quatermass Xperiment*, came at a difficult time for the British film industry when finance was in short supply, and as it took time for the returns to come in, Hammer embarked on a number of shorts. Apart from one or two dramatic items (like Joseph Losey's **A Man on the Beach**, a 29-minute

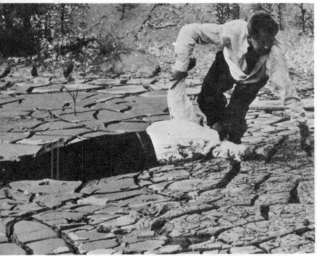

A Man on the Beach: Michael Ripper (body), Michael Medwin.

thriller), these were mainly travelogues or musicals and usually enhanced by colour and 'scope, the latter then very much a bonus for audiences used to black and white in British supporting films. Hollywood's big pictures were often so long that these short fillers found a ready place. 1956 also produced the last of the Anglo-American minor co-productions, **Women Without Men**, a prison story with humour and thrills but no big stars. Hammer tried a contribution to the ranks of British war films with Michael Carreras directing **The Steel Bayonet** (1957), the story of a battle-weary company holding a position

against enemy attack in Tunis in 1943 which was enlivened by excellent battle scenes spread across the wide screen in a process called Hammerscope and which also had the comparative novelty of letting the Germans speak their own language with subtitles.

It was another war film, however, that made a really startling impression: **The Camp on Blood Island** (1958). This dared to depict the kind of atrocities that were committed against British prisoners of war, portraying the Japanese as uncompromisingly brutal and arrogant. This film was accused of sensationalism —

The Camp on Blood Island.

perhaps with justice — but was a needed antidote to the gentlemanly behaviour prevalent in other British war films, which usually aimed at a family audience and an avoidance of stirring up old rancours. The film was so successful that it eventually led to a sequel, **The Secret of Blood Island** (1965).

The Snorkel (1958) took Hammer into the area of the adult thriller with Mandy Miller playing the teenage child who believes that her stepfather (Peter Van Eyck) killed her mother and passed it off as suicide as well as

Also in 1959, a new version of **The Hound of the Baskervilles** with Peter Cushing as Sherlock Holmes and Andre Morell as Watson, provided Hammer with a classic story that had some horrific elements the company was well placed to put over with panache.

Ten Seconds to Hell (1959) was a rare example of Hammer being involved in a principally Hollywood undertaking. This post-war drama was one of several in which director Robert Aldrich cast Jack Palance

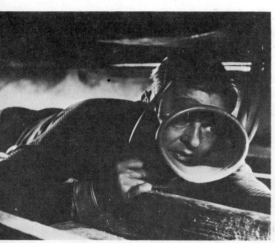

The Snorkel: Peter van Eyck.

murdering her father before that, making ingenious use of a piece of breathing apparatus, the snorkel. Her persistence in suspecting the stepfather soon places her own life in danger.

Comedy for (primarily) the domestic market was another feature of Hammer's activity with **Further Up The Creek** (1958) being a sequel to the successful **Up the Creek** and Frankie Howerd starring as the sailor who lets his ship out for luxury cruises while his commander isn't looking. Hammer also cashed in on the phenomenally successful TV series, "The Army Game", by transferring it to the big screen in **I Only Arsked** (1959).

Ten Seconds to Hell: Jack Palance.

against type in the hero's role and Jeff Chandler equally against expectations as the villain. Both are members of a bomb disposal unit intent on being the last survivor to claim the money the men have pooled, and the pair also quarrel over a glamorous German woman (Martine Carol). Hammer also took Bernard Bresslaw, the gawky comedian from "The Army Game" and *I only Arsked*, and put him in a comic treatment of the Jekyll and Hyde story, **The Ugly Duckling** (1959). Bresslaw plays a dim-witted descendant of the original Jekyll who rediscovers his grandfather's formula and turns himself into Teddy Hyde, gaining the confidence he lacked with his old personality and becoming a terror of the dance halls ·and a member of a jewel robbery outfit. Jerry Lewis later explored the same idea to more memorable effect in his *The Nutty Professor*.

It was through another war drama that Hammer again made a substantial impact, further breaking with genteel tradition by suggesting in **Yesterday's Enemy** (1959) that the British themselves were not always entirely honourable in war and capable of shooting two hostages in order to force information from another; this action was criticised by other British soldiers in the film as a war crime, and any necessary atonement was perhaps provided by the death of the British soldiers when they in turn were captured by the Japanese and refused to talk. Stanley Baker headed the cast under the direction of Val Guest who had made *Blood Island*.

Don't Panic Chaps! was another British comedy, adequate for its time, but **Never Take Sweets from a Stranger** (1960) was a potentially explosive drama on the subject of child molestation which, although given the distance of being set in Canada and exposing smalltown hypocrisy and corruption there,

The Ugly Duckling: Bernard Bresslaw.

Never Take Sweets from a Stranger:
Felix Aylmer, Janina Faye.

aroused fears that it might encourage what it set out to condemn. In the event, it was somewhat belatedly released without too much fuss as a second feature and proved an unprofitable enterprise that encouraged Hammer to "leave messages to Western Union" and merely entertain. This the company did very effectively in Val Guest's **Hell Is a City** (1960), an unusually tough crime thriller with some striking Manchester-area locations, starring Stanley Baker as the police inspector tracking down a jailbreaker who turns murderer (John Crawford) and coping with a frigid, nagging wife (Maxine Audley) who resents the time he spends on his work. Billie Whitelaw was involved in a moment of discreet nudity that was quite surprising for a British film of that period.

Hell is a City: Stanley Baker.

In 1961, **Visa to Canton** *(Passport to China)* featured the American actor Richard Basehart and was directed by Michael Carreras, **A Weekend With Lulu** and **Watch It Sailor**! were broad comedies that tickled many an undemanding rib and **Sword of Sherwood Forest** brought Richard Greene's TV Robin Hood to the big screen in colour. **Taste of Fear** *(Scream of Fear)* was a splendid exercise in squeezing thrills out of a cliché story (plot to drive young girl insane), well scripted by Jimmy Sangster, superbly photographed by Douglas Slocombe, and directed with dazzling

Weekend with Lulu: Leslie Phillips, Shirley Eaton, Irene Handl.

A Taste of Fear: Susan Strasberg.

skill for the precisely right effect by
Seth Holt. Hammer gave the film an
added boost by one of their most
effective selling gimmicks which con-
sisted of restricting publicity at the
time to a single still of the harassed
heroine, Susan Strasberg, screaming
her head off.

The Pirates of Blood River (1962),
The Scarlet Blade (*The Crimson
Blade*) (1963), **The Devil-Ship Pirates**
(1964) and **The Brigand of Kandahar**
(1965) were all costume adventures
with immediate appeal for young
audiences world-wide, two of them
featuring Christopher Lee as a colour-
ful pirate. Oliver Reed was also

The Devil-Ship Pirates: Ernest Clark, Christopher Lee.

The Scarlet Blade: Oliver Reed, Lionel Jeffries.

The Devil-Ship Pirates: Christopher Lee.

featured in three of them, as well as in Hammer's *The Damned* and *Curse of the Werewolf* discussed previously, but came into his own playing the title role in **Paranoiac** (1963) which, like the same year's **Maniac**, took Hammer into a brief and commercially disappointing phase of trying their hand at psychological thrillers that were dubbed "mini-Hitchcock" by Sir James Carreras.

Cash on Demand (1963) was an unusually compelling little thriller about a bank manager (Peter Cushing) forced to empty the vaults for a man (Andre Morell) who holds his family

hostage; told entirely without direct violence yet thick with the atmosphere of menace, it was inexplicably held back for a couple of years before quietly doing duty as a second feature, principally no doubt because of its short (66 minute) running time.

Nightmare (1964), like **Hysteria**, released the following year, was a well-made but unexceptional thriller without the extra elements of strong casting and horrific content that made the same period's *Fanatic* and *The Nanny* so much more appealing to the film-going audience.

It was in 1965 that Hammer first

She: Ursula Andress, Christopher Lee.

hit on the most successful alternative to making horror films with its remake of H. Rider Haggard's **She**. Although *Dr. No* had first enabled Ursula Andress to make her mark, it was in this film that she really achieved stardom, portraying Ayesha, the 2,000-year old queen of a secret tribe who lures young Leo Vincey (John Richardson) into her world, seeing in him the reincarnation of the lover she long ago murdered in a fit of jealousy. Cruel, arrogant, irresistible, Ayesha persuades Leo to bathe in the flame of eternal youth, with unfortunate results for both. With Miss Andress so much at the centre of things (and not looking a day over 25), those Hammer stalwarts, Christopher Lee and Peter Cushing, were for once thoroughly eclipsed.

Nothing indicates the success of a film more than a sequel and **The Vengeance of She** (1968) introduced a Czech actress, Olinka Berova, as the modern woman who is taken for the reincarnation of Ayesha by Killikrates (John Richardson), the murdered lover of the original *She* who this time round is the present day survivor rather than Ayesha. The sacred flame of immortality again burns bright, almost consuming the heroine and claiming Killikrates, who realises he has been mistaken in his belief that he has found Ayesha again.

One Million Years B.C. (1966), a remake of Hollywood's 1940 film of the same title, was publicised by Hammer as their 100th film, a claim approximately validated by the filmography in this book. This film gave a

The Vengeance of She: Olinka Berova.

One Million Years B.C.:
animation by Ray Harryhausen.

big starring opportunity to Raquel Welch after her promising work in *Fantastic Voyage*, casting her as one of the Shell people who chooses as a mate one of the Rock men (John Richardson). Ray Harryhausen's special effects competed for attention, creating the pterodactyl that carries the heroine off to drop her in the sea when engaged in sudden conflict. Freed of all but the most elementary dialogue, the film was a visual feast and one of Hammer's most pleasing ancient epics.

The Viking Queen (1967) came a little nearer the present day, with

The Viking Queen: Carita (centre).

Left: *One Million Years B.C.:* Raquel Welch, John Richardson.

Andrew Keir's tyrannical Roman invader of first century Britain being defeated by a woman, Salina (Carita), after he has flogged her in public and otherwise stirred dissent.

The Viking Queen: Andrew Keir, Carita.

A **Challenge** for **Robin Hood** (1967) was a minor production that provided good Christmas entertainment for family audiences in British cinemas while **Slave Girls** *(Prehistoric Women)* (1968) was a follow-up to the *She* kind of film with Martine Beswick as the queen of some dark-haired Amazon women who have conquered the local race of blondes and keep peace with the nearby men by donating the light-haired women to them. Miss Beswick also contributes

A Challenge for Robin Hood: Barry Ingham.

Slave Girls: Martine Beswick.

Slave Girls: Martine Beswick, Michael Latimer.

an enthusiastic dance display before the white hunter (Michael Latimer) who has fallen into her clutches.

Slave Girls.

Slave Girls: Michael Latimer, Martine Beswick.

Moon Zero Two: James Olson.

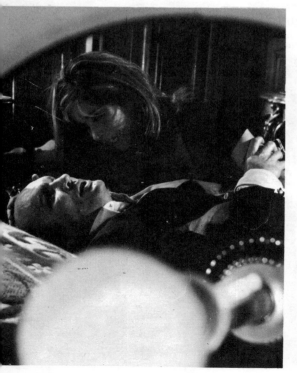

Crescendo: James Olson, Stefanie Powers.

Moon Zero Two (1969) might have opened up a whole new field of profitability for Hammer in the science-fiction *genre*; the company spent an unprecedented amount of money on it (£600,000) only to find that their story, labelled the "first space Western" and set fifty years in the future, could not match up to world interest in the real space landings that were taking place.

Crescendo (1970) also seemed to lack box-office impact. It was a psychological thriller with James Olson (who had starred in *Moon Zero Two*) and Stefanie Powers. As in *Fanatic*, the latter is faced with an insane woman, here the widow of a great composer intent on marrying off her son so that her late husband's talents may pass to future generations.

When Dinosaurs Ruled the Earth (1970) explored the same field as *One Million Years B.C.* and introduced Victoria Vetri as a member of the Rock Tribe who is rescued by a man from the Sea Tribe (Robin Hawdon) when she is blown into the ocean by a cyclone. Their fondness for each other makes them outcasts forced to battle against their fellow men, the elements,

When Dinosaurs Ruled the Earth: Victoria Vetri, Robin Hawdon.

and such creatures as a colossal snake, a man-eating cactus, and gigantic red ants in their efforts to stay alive. Miss Vetri had the looks but somehow failed to achieve the stardom that Ursula Andress and Raquel Welch had found in similar work for Hammer.

When Dinosaurs Ruled the Earth:
Victoria Vetri, Robin Hawdon.

When Dinosaurs Ruled the Earth: Victoria Vetri, Robin Hawdon.

When Dinosaurs Ruled the Earth: Victoria Vetri.

Creatures the World Forgot.

Creatures the World Forgot: Tony Bonner, Julie Ege.

Creatures the World Forgot: Tony Bonner, Julie Ege.

Creatures the World Forgot (1971) was Hammer's fourth excursion into the prehistoric past with Julie Ege as the daughter of a chief who is given to the leader of a rival tribe and learns to love him. Action is provided by the enmity between the leader (Tony Bonner) and his twin brother (Robert

Creatures the World Forgot: Marcia Fox.

Creatures the World Forgot.

John) who fight it out for control of the tribe on their father's death.

Since then, Hammer have found a cheaper way of achieving box-office success, joining the other British producers who have been making "spin-offs" or adaptations of popular TV series for the local cinema screen. As Hammer's past record shows, this was no new idea but only just recently have films with TV origins been made in such numbers as to be the virtual mainstay of the British film industry. Not all these latest "spin-offs" have succeeded and it is a tribute to Hammer's keen judgement that their first film, **On the Buses** (1971), should have been the outstanding hit of its year in British cinemas, reputedly

Creatures the World Forgot: Julie Ege.

On the Buses: Reg Varney, Michael Robbins, Anna Karen, Doris Hare.

On the Buses: Stephen Lewis, Reg Varney, Bob Grant.

Straight on till Morning: Shane Briant.

grossing more than one million pounds in its first six months of release. The plot had to do with women invading that sacred province of the male, the bus driving seat, in order to meet staffing problems, as well as domestic difficulties with hire purchase payments for some of the regular characters.

Though Hammer didn't neglect its horror output (as the filmography will show), and even tried its hand at a double suspense programme, *Fear in the Night* and *Straight On Till Morning* (1972), the success of *On the Buses* has stimulated the company into a whole series of "spin-offs". **Straight On Till Morning** gave a good acting opportunity to Shane Briant (of whom Hammer expect big things):

Straight on till Morning: Shane Briant, Rita Tushingham.

Fear in the Night: Judy Geeson.

Fear in the Night: Judy Geeson.

he appears as the psychotic murderer who befriends the plain girl from the provinces (Rita Tushingham), makes her pregnant, and plays to her tape recordings of his crimes. **Fear in the Night** was Jimmy Sangster's return to the *Taste of Fear* style of thriller with Judy Geeson as the girl who is driven out of her mind by the efforts of her husband (Ralph Bates) and his mistress (Joan Collins) who successfully coax her into shooting the latter's inconvenient husband (Peter Cushing).

Mutiny on the Buses (1972) was the inevitable sequel to *On the Buses*, the title deriving from a well-publicised competition. This time the bus crews were relocated in the

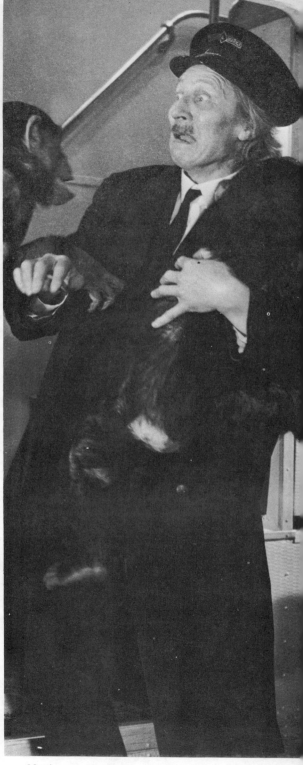

Mutiny on the Buses: Stephen Lewis.

country, with Stan (Reg Varney) making a disastrous trial run as driver of an excursion to Windsor Safari Park and the girls taking a ruling that they must only work in uniform so literally that they shed the knickers beneath them.

Mutiny on the Buses: Reg Varney, Janet Mahoney.

That's Your Funeral : Bill Fraser, Richard Wattis.

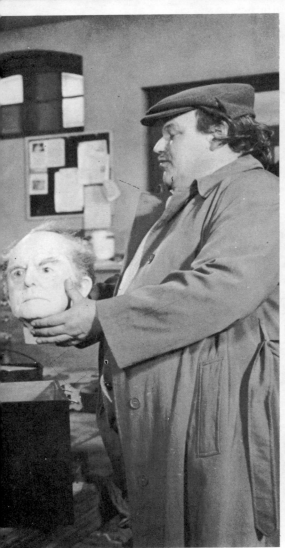

That's Your Funeral: Roy Kinnear.

That's Your Funeral, Love Thy Neighbour, Nearest and Dearest, Man at the Top and **Man About the House** proved that Hammer could no longer turn well-tried characters and situations into successful films. These comedies and sequels were no substitutes for Hammer's brilliance at chilling and thrilling cinema audiences.

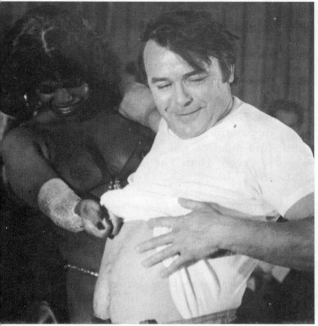

Love thy Neighbour: Princess Tamara, Jack Smethurst.   *Nearest and Dearest:* Hylda Baker, Jimmy Jewel.

Nearest and Dearest: Ed Malin, Hylda Baker, Madge Hindle, Jimmy Jewel.

ADAPT OR DIE

In the 1970s, the cult for vampire and monster movies peaked and died of a surfeit of horror and ruddy gore. For the time being, the audiences had enough of rot, fangs, beasts and breasts. Like an invasion of alien spores from another planet, Hammer's success had bred up hosts of lesser and cruder imitators, whose products killed off the market.

Public taste changed. Bruce Lee's lethal fists and feet brought in the era of Kung Fu's kicks and chops. Hammer tried to adapt to the new trend and died of it. Vampires should always travel towards the twilight, not towards the rising sun. Dracula did very well

going west to Whitby. It would have been the end of him going east to Hong Kong.

Michael Carreras, however, went east to Hong Kong to keep Hammer films alive. He agreed to make two pictures with the Shaw Brothers, the first one combining western vampires and oriental martial arts. The idea seemed excellent. In **The Legend of the 7 Golden Vampires**, a Chinese monk travelled alone to Dracula's tomb and was taken over by the Count's demonic presence. Chang Shen acted the transformation in a blood-curdling way, while the scene of the undead scrab-

NO ONE WAS SAFE AS LONG AS THIS *HEAD HUNTING THING* ROAMED THE LAND

NIGHT OF THE BLOOD BEAST

CERT X ADULTS ONLY

Starring MICHAEL EMMET · ANGELA GREENE · JOHN BAER

ANGLO AMALGAMATED FILM DISTRIBUTORS LTD

CINEVISION
présente

Un film de
SEX HORREUR

LE SADIQUE AUX DENTS ROUGES

avec
JANE CLAYTON
ALBERT SIMONO
DANIEL MOOSMANN
Mise en scène:
JEAN-LOUIS VAN BELLE
Musique:
RAYMOND LEGRAND
Editeur:
FONIOR
EN COULEURS
INTERDIT AUX MOINS DE 13 ANS

These posters advertise two of Hammer's lesser competitors.

bling from their graves, limping and whirling towards their prey and then galloping off on apocalyptic horses was one of the finest in the whole Hammer cycle.

Except for a clever sequence when David Chiang impaled a lecherous woman vampire and himself on the same stake, the combat sequences between Chinese villagers and powdery western vampires were neither Kung Fu nor convincing. Even Peter Cushing's invariable role as Van Helsing did not bridge the gap between Hammer and Hong Kong. Somewhere east of Mandalay, where the flying vampires

play, Dracula faded into the sunrise — and Hammer into the sunset.

The second of the Hong Kong co-productions, **Shatter**, was a routine action thriller starring Stuart Whitman. Michael Carreras himself had to take over the direction, but all the martial arts of Ti Lung could not pick up the pieces of this forced marriage between east and west. The twain simply did not meet except blow by blow.

A final foray into co-production in Germany with Christopher Lee starring in another Dennis Wheatley novel, **To the Devil a Daughter**, did not translate Hammer's gothic style to modern times

HAMMER HORROR!
DRAGON THRILLS!
The First
Kung Fu
Horror
Spectacular!

The Legend Of The
GOLDEN
VAMPIRES x

WARNER BROS.
A WARNER COMMUNICATIONS COMPANY PRESENTS
A HAMMER/SHAW PRODUCTION
THE LEGEND OF THE
"7 GOLDEN VAMPIRES" x
PETER CUSHING · JULIE EGE
DAVID CHIANG
ROBIN STUART/SHIH SZE TECHNICOLOR®/PANAVISION®

West meets East, not too successfully, in *The Legend of the 7 Golden Vampires.*

Mircalla (Yutte Stensgaard) gives the bite of death to her teacher (Ralph Bates) when he reveals that he knows she is the reincarnation of a famous vampire in *Lust for a Vampire*. The pose of the death kiss is almost religious.

 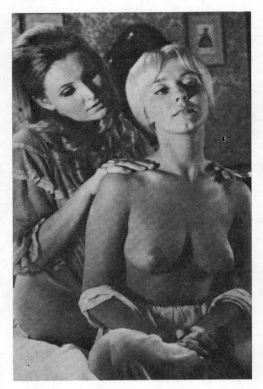

Another pupil at the girls' school (Pippa Steel) in *Lust for a Vampire* falls under the spell of Mircalla and begins to make love to her. Again, the scene is more suggestion than action, more dreamlike than erotic.

nor to the forests of Bavaria. Satan did not seem to relish flying east on Lufthansa any more than Dracula did on his trip to Cathay.

Hammer Films could not adapt to the cult of Kung Fu nor to the threat of television, which grew faster than an alien growth from "Quatermass" and blighted the cinemas of the land. But the final haemorrhage was the consequence of the financial crash of 1974, which put an end to most independent British film-making. After that, the future of Hammer would lie only in joining its old enemy, television, and in showing off its treasure trove to those nostalgic for the elegant gore of yesteryear.

Hammer had created a genre of English cinema that rivalled the success of the Ealing comedies. These two movie efflorescences were the only two schools of postwar British cinema that were successful internationally. What Peter Sellers and Alec Guinness were to Ealing, Christopher Lee and Peter Cushing were to Hammer. Lee made Dracula, as he said, into an aloof, dignified and austere figure, "exploding into tigerish activity when necessary." He refined even the blood-drinking, a gentleman to the tips of his fangs. "I nuzzle the victim," he said," . . . never kiss her on the lips. Then I mask what follows. It is more effective left to the imagination."

Seen against movern exploitation movies, the Hammer vampire films are remarkable for what they left to the

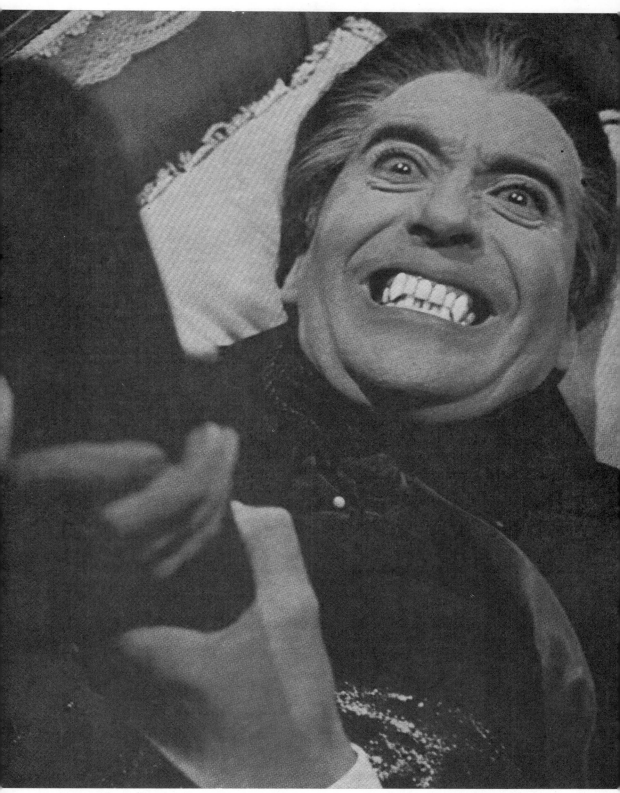

Christopher Lee removing the stake from his body in *Dracula Has Risen From the Grave*. He disapproved of the scene, but was over-ruled. "Everyone knows a stake through the heart is the very end of a vampire," he said. Not of him. Hammer needed Dracula to rise again.

Victoria Vetri menaced by giant pincers in *When Dinosaurs Ruled the Earth*.

Raquel Welch caught in the gigantic claws of a flying monster in *One Million Years B.C.*

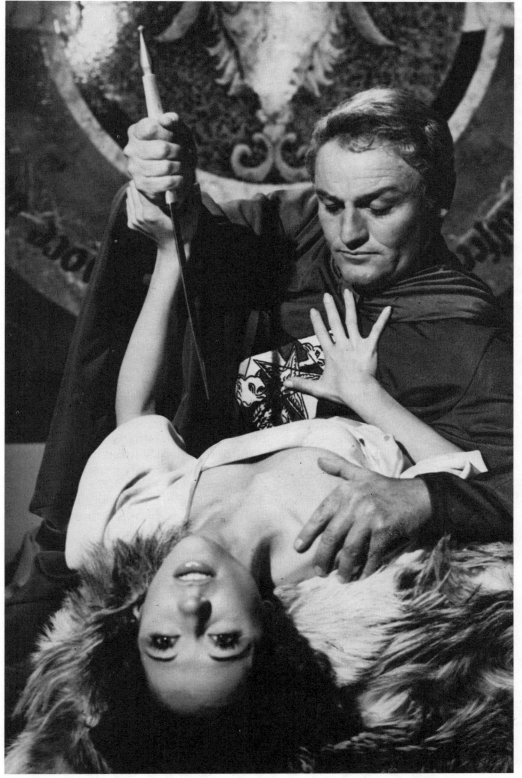

Charles Gray prepares to sacrifice Nike Arrighi to the powers of evil in *The Devil Rides Out*.

The bodysnatcher (Patrick Troughton) lifts the coffin lid to steal a corpse. More spare parts are needed for Frankenstein to make his Monster from Hell.

imagination. At the time, they may have seemed daubed with blood and studded with bosoms, but now they seem models of restraint and suggestion. There is a sense of ritual in them, a feeling for the subconscious and the unseen.

The taste of the vampire films did not extend to Hammer's comedy or fantasy films. In these, Hammer's directors often chose seaside vulgarity or a crude cartoon effect. Any young lady who found herself in Hammer's prehistoric times was liable to end up a Venus without furs, menaced by the antennae or jaws or claws of a magnified monster. Yet such excursions into neanderthal times had an engaging quality, a delight in elementary special effects which make them seem innocent and fresh after a surfeit of modern electronic gadgetry and big budget spectaculars. The low cost of the Hammer films always forced their directors to think imaginatively. In their cheapness lies much of their enduring charm.

Yet the images of Hammer films that will live forever in our minds are the gothic images of our European past. Bodysnatchers opening graves — monsters from our unconsciousness breaking down the barriers of our rational thoughts — beautiful bloodsuckers turning love into death — maidens under the sacrificial knife or in deadly peril — and even the image of our bodily corruption protruding into modern times. The pictures of Hammer films continue to haunt us wherever we may go. As long as we live, they cannot die.

So Hammer lives on. Although Michael Carreras has left, two of the film company's experienced producers and directors, Brian Lawrence and Roy Skeggs, have carried on the tradition by creating two series of television films. These have proved that Hammer still means the House of Horror. At twilight, on large screens and small, we can shiver to see that Hammer deserves the ancient epitaph

𝔑ot dead but liveth

Valerie Leon prepares to do away with another victim in *Blood from the Mummy's Tomb*.

Richard Wordsworth rots away with an unspeakable disease in *The Quatermass Xperiment*.

BRIDES OF DRACULA·AND OTHERS

Hammer's leading ladies

Stephanie Beacham

Ingrid Pitt

Veronica Carlson

Ursula Andress

Valerie Leon

Victoria Vetri

Edina Ronay

Martine Beswick

Joan Collins

Julie Ege

Olinka Berova

Susan Denberg

FILMOGRAPHY

This filmography is an attempt to list every film that has a place in the history of Hammer. It includes films produced by Hammer's parent company of the post-war period, Exclusive, since the same people were involved in both companies' productions, but excludes the films that Exclusive merely distributed from producers other than Hammer. Those Hammer films which were co-produced with other companies are so indicated immediately following the title and date and those made by Exclusive rather than Hammer are recorded in the same way; films where no production company credit is given after the title and date are Hammer productions completely.

The films are listed in their order of appearance in Britain and dates given are those of release, *not* production.

Credits are given in this order: director (*Dir:*), screenwriter (*Sc:*), director of photography (*Ph:*), production designer (*Prod. des:*), art director(s) (*Art dir:*), editor (*Ed:*) music composer (*Mus:*) (in some few cases, this may refer to the music director where no composer was credited), associate producer (*Assoc. prod:*), executive producer (*Exec. prod:*), producer (*Prod:*), distributor (*Rel:*), running time (mins) and colour and 'Scope where applicable. Then the cast, with the roles played by the principal actors indicated in italics after their names.

Where films are known to have been distributed in the United States, the name of the American distributor (where differing from the British) is given, and any major discrepancy in the year of American release is indicated along with the American distributor's name.

It remains to apologise to those many people whose diligent work in such departments as make-up, set decoration, and assistant direction we have been forced to exclude to keep this filmography to manageable dimensions. And, given the complexity and length of Hammer's history, it should be added that the odd film may have escaped the research net, although there should be no major omissions. In this respect, it might be noted that *Shadow of the Cat* and *Light Up the Sky*, two films that have been characterised as Hammer pictures, are in fact not productions of the company.

Even so, no detailed information has come to light on the following Hammer shorts: *The Seven Wonders of Ireland* (1957), *Ticket to Happiness* (1959), *Italian Holiday* (1957) (other than that it was directed by Peter Bryan), and *Highway Holiday* (1962) (other than it was produced and directed by Ian Lewis and made for Total Oil Products, ran 25 minutes, and dealt with an informal motor rally through Europe).

This filmography does not include Hammer's brief flirtations with TV. The enthusiastic help of Anthony Carreras and the Hammer staff in solving some of the vexing residual problems after principal research was completed is gratefully acknowledged. – A.E.

The Public Life of Henry the Ninth (1935)
Dir: Bernard Mainwaring. *Rel:* Metro-Goldwyn-Mayer. 60 mins.
With Leonard Henry (*Henry*), Betty Frankiss (*Maggie*), George Mozart (*Draughts Player*), Wally Patch (*Landlord*).

The Mystery of the Marie Celeste (1936)
[USA: **The Phantom Ship**]
Dir: Denison Clift. *Sc:* from a story by Denison Clift. *Ph:* Geoffrey Faithfull, Eric Cross. *Rel:* G.F.D. (Britain), Guaranteed (USA). 80 mins.

With Bela Lugosi (*Anton Lorenzen*), Shirley Grey (*Sarah Briggs*), Arthur Margaretson (*Captain Briggs*), Edmund Willard (*Toby Bilson*), George Mozart (*Tommy Duggan*), Ben Welden (*Boas Hoffman*), Dennis Hoey (*Tom Goodschard*), Gibson Gowland (*Andy Gillings*), Cliff McLaglen (*Captain Morehead*).

The Song of Freedom (1936)
Dir: J. Elder Wills. *Rel:* British Lion. 80 mins.
With Paul Robeson (*Zinga*), Elisabeth Welch (*Zinga's Wife*), Robert Adams (*Monty*), Cornelia Smith (*Queen Zinga*), Sydney Benson (*Gatekeeper*), Will Hammer (*Potman*), Alf Goddard (*Alf*), Ambrose Manning (*Trader*), George Mozart (*Bert Puddick*).

Sporting Love (1937)
Dir: J. Elder Wills. *Sc:* Fenn Sherie, Ingram D'Abbern, from a play by Stanley Lupino. *Ph:* Eric Cross. *Rel:* British Lion. 68 mins.
With Stanley Lupino (*Percy Brace*), Laddie Cliff (*Peter Brace*), Henry Carlisle (*Lord Dimsdale*), Eda Peel (*Maud Dane*), Bobby Comber (*Gerald Dane*).

River Patrol (1948)
A Knightsbridge—Hammer Production
Dir: Ben R. Hart. *Ph:* Brooks-Carrington. *Prod:* Hal Wilson. *Rel:* Exclusive. 46 mins.
With John Blythe (*Robby*), Wally Patch (*The Guy*), Lorna Dean (*Jean*), Stan Paskin.

Who Killed Van Loon? (1948)
An Exclusive Production
Rel: Exclusive. 48 mins.
With Raymond Lovell (*John Smith*), Kay Bannerman (*Dutch girl*), Robert Wyndham (*Scotland Yard policeman*).

Dick Barton, Special Agent (1948)
[USA TV: Dick Barton, Detective]
A Hammer—Marylebone Studios Production
Dir: Alfred Goulding. *Sc:* Alan Stranks, Alfred Goulding, from the BBC radio series. *Ph:* Stanley Clinton. *Rel:* Exclusive. 70 mins.
With Don Stannard (*Dick Barton*), George Ford (*Snowey*), Jack Shaw (*Jock*), Gillian Maude (*Jean*).

Dr. Morelle — The Case of the Missing Heiress (1949)
Dir: Godfrey Grayson. *Sc:* Roy Plomley, Ambrose Grayson, from the play by Wilfred Burr. *Ph:* Cedric Williams. *Art dir:* James Marchant. *Ed:* Ray Pitt. *Mus:* Frank Spencer, Rupert Grayson. *Prod:* Anthony Hinds. *Rel:* Exclusive. 73 mins.
With Valentine Dyall (*Dr. Morelle*), Julia Lang (*Miss Frayle*).

Dick Barton Strikes Back (1949)
An Exclusive Production

Dir: Godfrey Grayson. *Sc:* Ambrose Grayson, from the BBC radio series. *Ph:* Cedric Williams. *Rel:* Exclusive. 73 mins.
With Don Stannard (*Dick Barton*), Sebastian Cabot (*Fouracada*), Jean Lodge (*Tina*), James Raglan (*Lord Armadale*), Bruce Walker (*Snowey White*).

Celia (1949)
Dir: Francis Searle. *Sc:* A. R. Rawlinson, E. J. Mason, Francis Searle, from a BBC radio serial. *Ph:* Cedric Williams. *Mus:* Frank Spencer, Rupert Grayson. *Prod:* Anthony Hinds. *Rel:* Exclusive. 67 mins.
With Hy Hazell (*Celia*), Bruce Lester (*Larry*), John Bailey (*Lester Martin*), Elsie Wagstaff (*Aunt Nora*).

The Adventures of P.C.49 (1950)
Dir: Godfrey Grayson. *Sc:* Alan Stranks, Vernon Harris, from the BBC radio series. *Ph:* Cedric Williams. *Art dir:* James Marchant. *Ed:* Cliff Turner. *Mus:* Frank Spencer. *Prod:* Anthony Hinds. *Rel:* Exclusive. 67 mins.
With Hugh Latimer (*P.C. Archibald Berkeley Willoughby*), Patricia Cutts (*Joan*), John Penrose (*Barney*), Pat Nye (*Ma Brady*).

The Man in Black (1950)
Dir: Francis Searle. *Sc:* John Gilling, from a story by Francis Searle, based on a BBC radio series. *Ph:* Cedric Williams. *Art dir:* Denis Wreford. *Ed:* Ray Pitt. *Mus:* Frank Spencer. *Prod:* Anthony Hinds. *Rel:* Exclusive. 75 mins.
With Betty Ann Davies (*Bertha Clavering*), Sheila Burrell (*Janice*), Sidney James (*Henry Clavering/Hodson*), Anthony Forwood (*Victor Harrington*), Hazel Penwarden (*Joan*), Valentine Dyall (*Storyteller*).

Meet Simon Cherry (1950)
Dir: Godfrey Grayson. *Sc:* A. R. Rawlinson, Godfrey Grayson, with additional dialogue by Gale Pedrick, from a story by Godfrey Grayson based on the BBC radio series "Meet the Rev". *Ph:* Cedric Williams. *Art dir:* Denis Wreford. *Ed:* Ray Pitt. *Mus:* Frank Spencer. *Prod:* Anthony Hinds. *Rel:* Exclusive. 67 mins.
With Hugh Moxey (*Simon Cherry, "The Rev"*), Zena Marshall (*Lisa Colville*), Anthony Forwood (*Alan Colville*), John Bailey (*Henry Dantry*), Courtney Hope (*Lady Harling*), Jeanette Tregarthen (*Monica Harling*).

Room to Let (1950)
Dir: Godfrey Grayson. *Sc:* John Gilling, Godfrey Grayson, from the BBC feature by Margery Allingham. *Ph:* Cedric Williams. *Ed:* James Needs. *Mus:* Frank Spencer. *Prod:* Anthony Hinds. *Rel:* Exclusive. 68 mins.
With Jimmy Hanley (*Curly Minter*), Valentine Dyall (*Dr. Fell*), Christine Silver (*Mrs. Musgrave*), Merle Tottenham (*Alice*), Constance Smith (*Molly Musgrave*), Charles Hawtrey (*Mike Atkinson*), Aubrey Dexter (*Harding*).

Someone at the Door (1950)
Dir: Francis Searle. *Sc:* A. R. Rawlinson, from a play by Major Campbell Christie and Miss Dorothy Campbell Christie. *Ph:* Walter Harvey. *Art dir:* Denis Wreford. *Ed:* John Ferris. *Mus:* Frank Spencer. *Prod:* Anthony Hinds. *Rel:* Exclusive. 65 mins.
With Yvonne Owen (*Sally*), Michael Medwin (*Ronnie*), Hugh Latimer (*Bill*), Danny Green (*Price*), Gary Marsh (*Kapel*).

What the Butler Saw (1950)
Dir: Godfrey Grayson. *Sc:* A. R. Rawlinson, E. J. Mason, from a story by Roger and Donald Good. *Prod:* Anthony Hinds. *Rel:* Exclusive. 61 mins.
With Edward Rigby (*The Earl*), Mercy Haystead (*Lapis*), Henry Mollison (*Bembridge*), Michael Ward (*Gerald*), Peter Burton (*Bill Fenton*), Anne Valery (*Elaine*).

Dick Barton at Bay (1950)
Dir: Godfrey Grayson. *Sc:* Ambrose Grayson, from the BBC radio series. *Ph:* Stanley Clinton. *Art dir:* James Marchant. *Ed:* Max Brenner. *Mus:* Frank Spencer, Rubert Grayson. *Prod:* Henry Halstead. *Rel:* Exclusive. 68 mins.
With Don Stannard (*Dick Barton*), Tamara Desni (*Anna*), George Ford (*Snowey*), Meinhart Maur (*Serge Volkoff*), Joyce Linden (*Mary Mitchell*), Percy Walsh (*Professor Mitchell*), Campbell Singer (*Inspector Cavendish*).

The Lady Craved Excitement (1950)
Dir: Francis Searle. *Sc:* John Gilling, Edward J. Mason, Francis Searle, from a BBC serial by Edward J. Mason. *Ph:* Walter Harvey. *Ed:* John Ferris. *Mus:* Frank Spencer. *Songs:* James Dyrenforth, George Melachrino. *Prod:* Anthony Hinds. *Rel:* Exclusive. 69 mins.
With Hy Hazell (*Pat*), Michael Medwin (*Johnny*), Sidney James (*Carlo*), John Longden (*Inspector James*), Andrew Keir (*Peterson*), Danny Green (*Boris*) Thelma Grigg (*Julia*).

The Rossiter Case (1951)
Dir: Francis Searle. *Sc:* Kenneth Hyde, John Hunter, Francis Searle, from the play "The Rossiters" by Kenneth Hyde. *Ph:* Jimmy Harvey. *Ed:* John Ferris. *Mus:* Frank Spencer. *Prod:* Anthony Hinds. *Rel:* Exclusive. 75 mins.
With Helen Shingler (*Liz Rossiter*), Clement McCallin (*Peter*), Sheila Burrell (*Honor*), Frederick Leister (*Sir James Ferguson*), Ann Codrington (*Marty*), Henry Edwards (*Dr. Bendix*).

To Have and to Hold (1951)
Dir: Godfrey Grayson. *Sc:* Reginald Long, from the play by Lionel Brown. *Ph:* James Harvey. *Ed:* Jimmy Needs. *Mus:* Frank Spencer. *Prod:* Anthony Hinds. *Rel:* Exclusive. 63 mins.
With Avis Scott (*June*), Patrick Barr (*Brian

Harding*), Robert Ayres (*Max*), Harry Fine (*Robert*), Ellen Pollock (*Roberta*), Richard Warner (*Cyril*), Eunice Gayson, Peter Neil.

The Dark Light (1951)
An Exclusive Production
Dir: Vernon Sewell. *Sc:* Vernon Sewell. *Exec prod:* Anthony Hinds. *Prod:* Michael Carreras. *Rel:* Exclusive. 66 mins.
With Albert Lieven (*Mark*), David Greene (*Johnny*), Norman MacOwan (*Rigby*), Martin Benson (*Luigi*), Jack Stewart (*Matt*), Catherine Blake (*Linda*), Joan Carol (*Joan*).

Cloudburst (1951)
Dir: Francis Searle. *Sc:* Francis Searle, Leo Marks, from a story by Leo Marks. *Ph:* Walter Harvey. *Ed:* John Ferris. *Mus:* Frank Spencer. *Prod:* Anthony Hinds. *Rel:* Exclusive (Britain), United Artists (A Rudolph Monter Presentation) (USA). 92 mins. (Britain), 83 mins (USA).
With Robert Preston (*John Graham*), Elizabeth Sellars (*Carol Graham*), Colin Tapley (*Inspector Davis*), Sheila Burrell (*Lorna*), Harold Lang (*Mickie*).

The Black Widow (1951)
Dir: Vernon Sewell. *Sc:* Alan MacKinnon, from "Return to Darkness", a BBC serial by Lester Powell. *Ph:* Walter Harvey. *Ed:* James Needs. *Prod:* Anthony Hinds. *Rel:* Exclusive. 62 mins.
With Christine Norden (*Christine*), Robert Ayres (*Mark Sherwin*), Anthony Forwood (*Paul*), John Longden (*Kemp*), Jennifer Jayne (*Sheila*), John Harvey (*Dr. Wallace*).

A Case for P.C.49 (1951)
An Exclusive Production
Dir: Francis Searle. *Sc:* Alan Stranks, Vernon Harris, from the BBC radio series. *Ph:* Walter Harvey. *Mus:* Frank Spencer. *Prod:* Anthony Hinds. *Rel:* Exclusive (Britain), Lippert (USA).
With Brian Reece (*P.C.49*), Joy Shelton (*Joan Carr*), Christine Norden (*Della Dainton*), Leslie Bradley (*Palantine*), Gordon McLeod (*Inspector Wilson*), Campbell Singer (*Sergeant Wright*)

Death of an Angel (1952)
An Exclusive Production
Dir: Charles Saunders. *Sc:* Reginald Long, from the story "This Is Mary's Chair" by Frank King. *Ph:* Walter Harvey. *Ed:* John Ferris. *Mus:* Frank Spencer. *Prod:* Anthony Hinds. *Rel:* Exclusive. 64 mins.
With Patrick Barr (*Robert Welling*), Jane Baxter (*Mary Welling*), Julie Somers (*Judy Welling*), Raymond Young (*Christopher Boswell*), Jean Lodge (*Ann Marlow*), Russell Waters (*Walter Grannage*).

Whispering Smith Hits London (1952)
[USA: **Whispering Smith vs. Scotland Yard**]
Dir: Francis Searle. *Sc:* John Gilling, from a story
by Frank H. Spearman. *Ph:* Walter Harvey. *Ed:*
Jimmy Needs. *Mus:* Frank Spencer. *Prod:* Anthony
Hinds. *Rel:* Exclusive (Britain), RKO Radio (USA).
82 mins (Britain), 77 mins (USA).
With Richard Carlson (*Whispering Smith*), Greta
Gynt (*Louise*), Herbert Lom (*Ford*), Rona
Anderson (*Anne*), Alan Wheatley (*Reith*), Dora
Bryan (*La Fosse*), Reginald Beckwith (*Manson*).

The Last Page (1952)
[USA: **Man Bait**]
An Exclusive—Lippert Production
Dir: Terence Fisher. *Sc:* Frederick Knott, from a
novel by James Hadley Chase. *Ph:* Walter Harvey.
Ed: Maurice Rootes. *Mus:* Frank Spencer. *Prod:*
Anthony Hinds. *Rel:* Exclusive (Britain), Lippert
(USA). 84 mins (Britain), 78 mins (USA).
With George Brent (*John Harman*), Marguerite
Chapman (*Stella*), Raymond Huntley (*Clive*), Peter
Reynolds (*Jeff*), Diana Dors (*Ruby*), Eleanor
Summerfield (*Vi*), Meredith Edwards (*Dale*), Harry
Fowler (*Joe*).

Never Look Back (1952)
An Exclusive Production
Dir: Francis Searle. *Sc:* John Hunter, Guy Morgan,
Francis Searle. *Ph:* Reginald Wyer. *Art dir:* Alec
Gray. *Ed:* John Ferris. *Mus:* Temple Abady. *Prod:*
Michael Carreras. *Rel:* Exclusive. 73 mins.
With Rosamund John (*Anne Maitland, KC*), Hugh
Sinclair (*Nigel Stuart*), Guy Middleton (*Guy
Ransom*), Henry Edwards (*Whitcomb*), Terence
Longdon (*Alan*), John Warwick (*Raynor*), Brenda
de Banzie (*Molly Wheeler*).

Wings of Danger (1952)
Dir: Terence Fisher. *Sc:* John Gilling. from a story
by Elleston Trevor and Packham Webb. *Ph:* Walter
Harvey. *Ed:* Jim Needs. *Mus:* Malcolm Arnold.
Prod: Anthony Hinds. *Rel:* Exclusive (Britain),
Lippert (USA). 73 mins.
With Zachary Scott (*Van*), Robert Beatty (*Nick
Talbot*), Kay Kendall (*Alexia*), Naomi Chance
(*Avril*), Arthur Lane (*Boyd Spencer*), Colin Tapley
(*Maxwell*), Diane Cilento (*Jeannette*), Harold Lang.

Stolen Face (1952)
An Exclusive Production
Dir: Terence Fisher. *Sc:* Richard H. Landau,
Martin Berkeley. *Ph:* Walter Harvey. *Ed:* Maurice
Rootes. *Mus:* Malcolm Arnold. *Prod:* Michael
Hinds. *Rel:* Exclusive (Britain), Lippert (USA).
72 mins.
With Paul Henreid (*Dr. Philip Ritter*), Lizabeth
Scott (*Alice Brent/Lily B*), Mary Mackenzie (*Lily
A*), Andre Morell (*David*), John Wood (*Dr. Jack
Wilson*), Susan Stephen (*Betty*).

Lady in the Fog (1952)
[USA: **Scotland Yard Inspector**]
Dir: Sam Newfield. *Sc:* Orville H. Hampton, from
the BBC serial by Lester Powell. *Ph:* Jimmy
Harvey. *Art dir:* Wilfred Arnold. *Ed:* Jimmy Needs.
Prod: Anthony Hinds. *Rel:* Exclusive (Britain),
Lippert (USA). 82 mins (Britain), 73 mins (USA).
With Cesar Romero (*Philip Odell*), Lois Maxwell
(*Peggy*), Bernadette O'Farrell (*Heather*), Geoffrey
Keen (*Hampden*), Campbell Singer (*Inspector
Rigby*), Alastair Hunter (*Sergeant Reilly*), Mary
Machenzie (*Marilyn*)

Mantrap (1952)
[USA: **Man in Hiding**]
An Exclusive Production
Dir: Terence Fisher. *Sc:* Paul Tabori, Terence
Fisher, from a novel *Queen in Danger* by Elleston
Trevor. *Ph:* Reginald Wyer. *Art dir:* Elder Wills.
Ed: Jim Needs. *Mus:* Doreen Carwithen. *Prod:*
Michael Carreras, Alexander Paal. *Rel:* Exclusive
(Britain), United Artists (USA). 79 mins.
With Paul Henreid (*Hugo Bishop*), Lois Maxwell
(*Thelma*), Kieron Moore (*Speight*), Hugh Sinclair
(*Jerrard*), Lloyd Lamble (*Frisnay*), Anthony
Forwood (*Rex*), Bill Travers (*Victor*), Mary Laura
Wood (*Susie*), Kay Kendall (*Vera*).

The Gambler and the Lady (1953)
An Exclusive Production
Dir: Pat Jenkins*/Terence Fisher†. *Ph:* Walter
Harvey. *Art dir:* J. Elder Wills. *Ed:* Maurice
Rootes. *Mus:* Ivor Slaney. *Prod:* Anthony Hinds.
Rel: Exclusive (Britain), Lippert (USA, 1952).
74 mins (Britain), 71 mins (USA).
With Dane Clark (*Jim Forster*), Kathleen Byron
(*Pat*), Naomi Chance (*Susan Willens*), Meredith
Edwards (*Dave*), Anthony Forwood (*Peter
Willens*), Eric Pohlmann (*Arturo Colonna*).
* American sources credit Sam Newfield with
co-direction.
† While contemporary sources give Pat Jenkins,
more recent sources credit Terence Fisher.

Four-Sided Triangle (1953)
Dir: Terence Fisher. *Sc:* Paul Tabori, Terence
Fisher, from a novel by William F. Temple. *Ph:*
Reginald Wyer. *Art dir:* J. Elder Wills. *Ed:* Maurice
Rootes. *Mus:* Malcolm Arnold. *Prod:* Michael
Carreras, Alexander Paal. *Rel:* Exclusive (Britain),
Astor (USA). 81 mins.
With Barbara Payton (*Lena/Helen*), James Hayter
(*Dr. Harvey*), Stephen Murray (*Bill*), John Van
Eyssen (*Robin*), Percy Marmont (*Sir Walter*).

Spaceways (1953)
Dir: Terence Fisher. *Sc:* Paul Tabori, Richard
Landau, from a radio play by Charles Eric Maine.
Ph: Reginald Wyer. *Art dir:* J. Elder Wills. *Ed:*
Maurice Rootes. *Mus:* Ivor Slaney. *Prod:* Michael
Carreras. *Rel:* Exclusive (Britain), Lippert (USA).
76 mins.

With Howard Duff (*Stephen Mitchell*), Eva Bartok (*Lisa Frank*), Andrew Osborn (*Philip Crenshaw*), Anthony Ireland (*General Hays*), Alan Wheatley (*Smith*), Michael Medwin (*Toby Andrews*).

The Flanagan Boy (1953)
[USA: **Bad Blonde**]
An Exclusive Production
Dir: Reginald LeBorg. *Sc:* Guy Elmes, Richard Landau, from the novel by Max Catto. *Ph:* Walter Harvey. *Art dir:* Wilfred Arnold. *Ed:* James Needs. *Mus:* Ivor Slaney. *Prod:* Anthony Hinds. *Rel:* Exclusive (Britain), Lippert (USA). 81 mins.
With Barbara Payton (*Lorna*), Tony Wright (*Johnny Flanagan*), Fredrick Valk (*Giuseppe Vecchi*), John Slater (*Charlie*), Sidney James (*Sharkey*), Marie Burke (*Mrs. Vecchi*).

The Saint's Return (1953)
[USA: **The Saint's Girl Friday**]
Dir: Seymour Friedman. *Sc:* Allan MacKinnon, from characters created by Leslie Charteris. *Ph:* Walter Harvey. *Art dir:* J. Elder Wills. *Ed:* James Needs. *Mus:* Ivor Slaney. *Prod:* Anthony Hinds, Julian Lesser. *Rel:* Exclusive (Britain), RKO Radio (USA). 73 mins (Britain), 68 mins (USA).
With Louis Hayward (*Simon Templar, "The Saint"*), Sydney Tafler (*Max Lennar*), Naomi Chance (*Lady Carol Denbeigh*), Charles Victor (*Chief Inspector Teal*), Diana Dors (*Margie*), Harold Lang (*Jarvis*).

Face the Music (1954)
[USA: **The Black Glove**]
Dir: Terence Fisher. *Sc:* Ernest Borneman, from his novel. *Ph:* Jimmy Harvey. *Art dir:* J. Elder Wills. *Ed:* Maurice Rootes. *Mus:* Ivor Slaney, Kenny Baker. *Prod:* Michael Carreras. *Rel:* Exclusive (Britain), Lippert (USA). 84 mins.
With Alex Nicol (*James Bradley*), Eleanor Summerfield (*Barbara Quigley*), John Salew (*Max Margulis*), Paul Carpenter (*Johnny Sutherland*), Geoffrey Keen (*Maurice Green*), Ann Hanslip (*Maxine*).

Blood Orange (1954)
[USA: **Three Stops to Murder**]
Dir: Terence Fisher. *Sc:* Jan Read. *Ph:* Jimmy Harvey. *Art dir:* J. Elder Wills. *Ed:* Maurice Rootes. *Mus:* Ivor Slaney. *Prod:* Michael Carreras. *Rel:* Exclusive (Britain), Astor (USA). 76 mins.
With Tom Conway (*Tom Conway*), Mila Parely (*Helen Pascal*), Naomi Chance (*Gina*), Eric Pohlmann (*Mercedes*), Andrew Osborn (*Captain Simpson*).

Life with the Lyons (1954)
An Exclusive Production
Dir: Val Guest. *Sc:* Val Guest, Robert Dunbar, from the BBC radio series. *Ph:* Walter Harvey. *Art dir:* Wilfred Arnold. *Ed:* Doug Myers. *Mus:* Arthur

Wilkinson. *Prod:* Robert Dunbar. *Rel:* Exclusive. 81 mins.
With Ben Lyon, Bebe Daniels, Barbara Lyon, Richard Lyon (*Themselves*), Hugh Morton (*Mr. Hemmingway*) Horace Percival (*Wimple*), Molly Weir (*Aggie*), Doris Rogers (*Florrie*), Gwen Lewis (*Mrs. Wimple*), Arthur Hill (*Slim Cassidy*), Belinda Lee (*Violet*).

The House across the Lake (1954)
[USA: **Heat Wave**]
Dir: Ken Hughes. *Sc:* Ken Hughes, from his novel *High Wray*. *Ph:* James Harvey. *Art dir:* J. Elder Wills. *Ed:* James Needs. *Mus:* Ivor Slaney. *Prod:* Anthony Hinds. *Rel:* Associated British-Pathe (Britain), Lippert (USA). 68 mins.
With Alex Nicol (*Mark Kendrick*), Hillary Brooke (*Carol Forrest*), Susan Stephen (*Andrea Forrest*), Sidney James (*Beverley Forrest*), Alan Wheatley (*Inspector Maclennan*), Paul Carpenter (*Vincent Gordon*).

The Stranger Came Home (1954)
[USA: **The Unholy Four**]
Dir: Terence Fisher. *Sc:* Michael Carreras, from the novel *Stranger at Home* by George Sanders. *Ph:* James Harvey. *Art Dir:* Jim Elder Wills. *Ed:* Bill Lenney. *Mus:* Ivor Slaney. *Prod :* Michael Carreras. *Rel :* Exclusive (Britain), Lippert (USA). 80 mins.
With Paulette Goddard (*Angie*), William Sylvester (*Philip Vickers*), Patrick Holt (*Job Crandall*), Paul Carpenter (*Bill Saul*), Alvys Mahen (*Joan Merrill*), Russell Napier (*Inspector Treherne*), David King Wood (*Sessions*).

Five Days (1954)
[USA: **Paid to Kill**]
Dir: Montgomery Tully. *Sc:* Paul Tabori. *Ph:* Jimmy Harvey. *Art dir:* J. Elder Wills. *Ed:* James Needs. *Mus:* Ivor Slaney. *Prod:* Anthony Hinds. *Rel:* Exclusive (Britain), Lippert (USA). 72 mins.
With Dane Clark (*Nevill*), Paul Carpenter (*Paul*), Thea Gregory (*Andrea*), Cecile Chevreau (*Joan*), Anthony Forwood (*Glanville*), Howard Marion Crawford (*McGowan*).

36 Hours (1954)
[USA: **Terror Street**]
Dir: Montgomery Tully. *Sc:* Steve Fisher. *Ph:* Jimmy Harvey. *Art dir:* J. Elder Wills. *Prod:* Tony Hinds. *Rel:* Exclusive (Britain), Lippert (USA). 80 mins (Britain), 84 mins (USA).
With Dan Duryea (*Bill*), Elsy Albiin (*Katie*), John Chandos (*Orville Hart*), Ann Gudrun (*Jenny*), Eric Pohlmann (*Slauson*), Kenneth Griffith (*Henry*), Jane Carr (*Sister Helen-Clair*).

Men of Sherwood Forest (1954)
Dir: Val Guest. *Sc:* Allan Mackinnon. *Ph:* Jimmy Harvey. *Art dir:* Jim Elder Wills. *Ed:* Jim Needs. *Mus:* Doreen Corwithen. *Prod:* Michael Carreras.

Rel: Exclusive (Britain), Astor (USA). 77 mins. Eastman Colour.
With Don Taylor (*Robin Hood*), Reginald Beckwith (*Friar Tuck*), Eileen Moore (*Lady Alys*), David King Wood (*Sir Guy Belton*), Douglas Wilmer (*Sir Nigel Saltire*), Harold Lang (*Hubert*), Leslie Linder (*Little John*), John Van Eyssen (*Will Scarlet*), Patrick Holt (*King Richard, Coeur de Lion*).

Mask of Dust (1954)
[USA: **A Race for Life**]
Dir: Terence Fisher. *Sc:* Richard Landau, from the novel by Jon Manchip White. *Ph:* Jimmy Harvey. *Art dir:* Jim Elder Wills. *Ed:* Bill Lenny. *Mus:* Leonard Salzedo. *Exec. prod:* Michael Carreras. *Prod:* Mickey Delamar. *Rel:* Exclusive (Britain), Lippert (USA). 79 mins (Britain), 69 mins (USA).
With Richard Conte (*Peter Wells*), Mari Aldon (*Pat Wells*), George Coulouris (*Dallapiccola*), Peter Illing (*Bollario*).

The Lyons in Paris (1955)
Dir: Val Guest. *Sc:* Val Guest, from the characters of the BBC radio series. *Ph:* Jimmy Harvey. *Art dir:* Wilfred Arnold. *Ed:* Doug Myers. *Mus:* Bruce Campbell. *Prod:* Robert Dunbar. *Rel:* Exclusive. 81 mins.
With Ben Lyon, Bebe Daniels Lyon, Barbara Lyon, Richard Lyon (*Themselves*), Horace Percival (*Mr. Wimple*), Molly Weir (*Aggie*), Doris Rogers (*Florrie*), Gwen Lewis (*Mrs. Wimple*), Hugh Morton (*Colonel Price*), Reginald Beckwith (*Captain Le Grand*), Martine Alexis (*Fifi la Fleur*).

Break in the Circle (1955)
Dir: Val Guest. *Sc:* Val Guest, from a novel by Philip Lorraine. *Ph:* Walter Harvey. *Art dir:* J. Elder Wills. *Ed:* Bill Lenny. *Mus:* Doreen Corwithen. *Assoc. prod:* Mickey Delamar. *Prod:* Michael Carreras. *Rel:* Exclusive (Britain), 20th Century-Fox (USA, 1957). 91 mins (Britain), 69 mins (USA). Eastman Colour (black and white in USA).
With Forrest Tucker (*Skip Morgan*), Eva Bartok (*Lisa*), Marius Goring (*Baron Keller*), Eric Pohlmann (*Emile*), Guy Middleton (*Hobart*), Arnold Marlé (*Kudnic*), Fred Johnson (*Farquarson*), David King Wood (*Patchway*), Reginald Beckwith (*Dusty*).

Third Party Risk (1955)
[USA: **Deadly Game**, released to TV as **Big Deadly Game**]
Dir: Daniel Birt. *Sc:* Daniel Birt, Robert Dunbar, from a novel by Nicolas Bentley. *Ph:* Jimmy Harvey. *Art dir:* Jim Elder Wills. *Ed:* James Needs. *Mus:* Michael Krein. *Prod:* Robert Dunbar. *Rel:* Exclusive (Britain), Lippert (USA). 70 mins (Britain), 63 mins (USA).
With Lloyd Bridges (*Philip Graham*), Finlay Currie (*Darius*), Maureen Swanson (*Lolita*), Simon Silva (*Mitzi*), Ferdy Mayne (*Maxwell Carey*).

Murder by Proxy (1955)
[USA: **Blackout**]
An Exclusive Production
Dir: Terence Fisher. *Sc:* Richard Landau, from the novel by Helen Nielsen. *Ph:* Jimmy Harvey. *Art dir:* Jim Elder Wills. *Ed:* Maurice Rootes. *Mus:* Ivor Slaney. *Prod:* Michael Carreras. *Rel:* Exclusive (Britain), Lippert (USA, 1954). 87 mins.
With Dane Clark (*Casey Morrow*), Belinda Lee (*Phyllis Brunner*), Eleanor Summerfield (*Maggie Doone*), Andrew Osborn (*Lance Gordon*), Betty Ann Davies (*Alicia Brunner*).

Cyril Stapleton and the Show Band (1955)
Dir: Michael Carreras. *Prod:* Michael Carreras. *Rel:* Exclusive. 29 mins. Eastman Colour. CinemaScope.
With Cyril Stapleton and the Show Band, Lita Roza, Ray Burns.
(Musical featurette).

The Glass Cage (1955)
[USA: **The Glass Tomb**]
Dir: Montgomery Tully. *Sc:* Richard Landau, from a novel by A.E. Martin. *Ph:* Walter Harvey. *Art dir:* J. Elder Wills. *Ed:* James Needs. *Mus:* Leonard Salzedo. *Prod:* Anthony Hinds. *Rel:* Exclusive (Britain), Lippert (USA). 59 mins.
With John Ireland (*Pel*), Honor Blackman (*Jenny*), Geoffrey Keen (*Stanton*), Eric Pohlmann (*Sapolio*), Sidney James (*Tony Lewis*), Liam Redman (*Lindley*).

The Eric Winstone Band Show (1955)
Dir: Michael Carreras. *Prod:* Michael Carreras. *Rel:* Exclusive. 30 mins. Eastman Colour. CinemaScope.
With Alma Cogan, Eric Winstone and his Orchestra, Kenny Baker, The George Mitchell Singers.
(Musical featurette.)

The Quatermass Xperiment (1955)
[USA: **The Creeping Unknown**]
Dir: Val Guest. *Sc:* Richard Landau, Val Guest, from the BBC TV serial "The Quatermass Experiment" by Nigel Kneale. *Ph:* Walter Harvey. *Art dir:* J. Elder Wills. *Ed:* James Needs. *Special effects:* Leslie Bowie. *Mus:* James Bernard. *Prod:* Anthony Hinds. *Rel:* Exclusive (Britain), United Artists (USA, 1956). 82 mins (Britain), 78 mins (USA).
With Brian Donlevy (*Bernard Quatermass*), Jack Warner (*Inspector Lomax*), Margia Dean (*Judith Carroon*), Richard Wordsworth (*Victor Carroon*), David King Wood (*Gordon Briscoe*), Thora Hird (*Rosie*), Gordon Jackson (*TV producer*).

The Right Person (1955)
Dir: Peter Cotes. *Sc:* from a story by Philip Mackie. *Ph:* Walter Harvey. *Ed:* Spencer Reeve. *Mus:* Eric Winstone. *Assoc prod:* Mickey Delamar. *Prod:* Michael Carreras. *Rel:* Exclusive. 30 mins. Eastman Colour. CinemaScope.
With Margo Lorenz, Douglas Wilmer, David Markham.

Just for You (1956)
Dir: Michael Carreras. *Prod:* Michael Carreras. *Rel:*
Exclusive. Eastman Colour. CinemaScope.
With Cyril Stapleton and the Show Band, The
Show Band Singers, Joan Regan, Ronnie Harris.
(Musical featurette.)

A Man on the Beach (1956)
Dir: Joseph Losey. *Sc:* Jimmy Sangster, from the
story "Chance at the Wheel" by Victor Canning.
Ph: Wilkie Cooper. *Art dir:* Edward Marshall. *Ed:*
Henry Richardson. *Mus:* John Hotchkis. *Prod:*
Anthony Hinds. *Rel:* Exclusive. 29 mins. Eastman
Colour. Cinepanoramic.
With Donald Wolfit (*Carter*), Michael Medwin
(*Max*), Michael Ripper (*Chauffeur*), Alex de Gallier
(*Casino Manager*), Edward Forsyth (*Clement*).

Parade of the Bands (1956)
Dir: Michael Carreras. *Prod:* Michael Carreras. *Rel:*
Exclusive. 30 mins. Eastman Colour. CinemaScope.
With Malcolm Mitchell and his Orchestra, Eric
Jupp and his Players, Freddy Randall and his Band,
Frank Weir and his Orchestra with Liza Ashwood
and Rusty Hurran, Johnny Dankworth and his
Orchestra with Cleo Laine, Francisco Cavez and his
Latin American Orchestra.
(Musical featurette.)

Eric Winstone's Stagecoach (1956)
Dir: Michael Carreras. *Ph:* Geoffrey Unsworth. *Art
dir:* Edward Marshall. *Ed:* James Needs. *Prod:*
Michael Carreras. 30 mins. Eastman Colour.
HammerScope.
With Eric Winstone and his Orchestra, Alma Cogan,
Marion Ryan, Ray Ellington Quartet.
(Musical featurette.)

Women Without Men (1956)
Dir: Elmo Williams. *Sc:* Val Guest, Richard
Landau. *Ph:* Walter Harvey. *Art dir:* John Elphick.
Ed: James Needs. *Mus:* Leonard Salzedo. *Prod:*
Anthony Hinds. *Rel:* Exclusive. 73 mins.
With Beverley Michaels (*Angie Booth*), Joan Rice
(*Cleo*), Thora Hird (*Granny*), Paul Carpenter
(*Nick*), Avril Angers (*Bessie*), Ralph Michael
(*Julian*), April Olrich (*Marguerite*), Eugene Deckers
(*Pierre*), Gordon Jackson (*Percy*).

Copenhagen (1956)
Dir: Michael Carreras. *Ph:* Len Harris. *Ed:* Bill
Lenny. *Mus:* Eric Winstone. *Prod:* Michael
Carreras. 16 mins. Eastman Colour. CinemaScope.
Tom Conway (*Commentator*).
(Travelogue.)

X the Unknown (1956)
Dir: Leslie Norman. *Sc:* Jimmy Sangster. *Ph:*
Gerald Gibbs. *Ed:* James Needs. *Special effects:*

Jack Curtis, Bowie Margutti Ltd. *Mus:* James
Bernard. *Prod:* Anthony Hinds. *Rel:* Exclusive
(Britain), Warner Bros. (USA, 1957). 78 mins.
With Dean Jagger (*Dr. Adam Royston*), Edward
Chapman (*Elliott*), Leo McKern (*McGill*), William
Lucas (*Peter*), John Harvey (*Major Cartwright*),
Peter Hammond (*Lt. Bannerman*).

Dick Turpin — Highwayman (1956)
Dir: David Paltenghi. *Sc:* Joel Murcott. *Ph:*
Stephen Dade. *Art dir:* Ted Marshall. *Ed:* James
Needs. *Prod:* Michael Carreras. 22 mins. Eastman
Colour. HammerScope.
With Philip Friend (*Dick Turpin*), Diane Hart (*Liz*),
Allan Cuthbertson (*Jonathan Redgrove*), Gabrielle
May (*Genevieve*).

The Edmundo Ros Half Hour (1957)
Dir: Michael Carreras. *Ph:* Geoffrey Unsworth. *Art
dir:* Edward Marshall. *Ed:* James Needs. *Assoc.
prod:* Mickey Delamar. *Prod:* Michael Carreras.
Rel: Exclusive. 30 mins. Eastman Colour.
HammerScope.
With The Edmundo Ros Latin American Orchestra,
Ines Del Carmen, Morton Frazer's Harmonica
Gang, The Buddy Bradley Dancers, Elizabeth
Shelley.
(Musical featurette.)

The Curse of Frankenstein (1957)
Dir: Terence Fisher. *Sc:* Jimmy Sangster, from the
story by Mary Bysshe Shelley. *Ph:* Jack Asher. *Art
dir:* Ted Marshall. *Ed:* James Needs. *Mus:* James
Bernard. *Exec. prod:* Michael Carreras. *Assoc.
prod:* Anthony Nelson-Keys. *Prod:* Anthony
Hinds. *Rel:* Warner Bros. 82 mins. Eastman Colour.
With Peter Cushing (*Baron Victor Frankenstein*),
Christopher Lee (*The Creature*), Hazel Court
(*Elizabeth*), Robert Urquhart (*Paul Krempe*),
Valerie Gaunt (*Justine*), Noel Hood (*Aunt Sophia*),
Melvyn Hayes (*The Young Victor*), Paul
Hardtmuth (*Prof. Bernstein*).

The Steel Bayonet (1957)
Dir: Michael Carreras. *Sc:* Howard Clewes. *Ph:*
Jack Asher. *Art dir:* Ted Marshall. *Ed:* Bill Lenny.
Mus: Leonard Salzedo. *Assoc. prod:* Anthony
Nelson-Keys. *Prod:* Michael Carreras. *Rel:* United
Artists. 85 mins. Hammerscope.
With Leo Genn (*Major Gerrard*), Kieron Moore
(*Captain Mead*), Michael Medwin (*Lt. Vernon*),
Robert Brown (*Sgt.-Major Gill*), Michael Ripper
(*Private Middleditch*).

Quatermass II (1957)
[USA: **Enemy from Space**]
Dir: Val Guest. *Sc:* Val Guest, Nigel Kneale, from
the BBC TV serial by Nigel Kneale. *Ph:* Gerald
Gibbs. *Art dir:* Bernard Robinson. *Ed:* Jim Needs.
Mus: James Bernard. *Exec. prod:* Michael Carreras.
Prod: Anthony Hinds. *Rel:* United Artists.
85 mins.

With Brian Donlevy (*Professor Quatermass*), John Longden (*Lomax*), Sidney James (*Jimmy Hall*), Bryan Forbes (*Marsh*), William Franklyn (*Brand*), Vera Day (*Sheila*), Charles Lloyd Pack (*Dawson*), Tom Chatto (*Broadhead*), John Van Eyssen (*The PRO*), Percy Herbert (*Gorman*).

Day of Grace (1957)
Dir: Francis Searle. *Sc:* Jon Manchip White, Francis Searle. *Ph:* Denny Densham. *Art dir:* Bernard Robinson. *Ed:* Bill Lenny, Stanley Smith. *Prod:* Francis Searle. *Rel:* Exclusive. 26 mins. Eastman Colour. HammerScope.
With Vincent Winter (*Ian*), John Lawrie (*Uncle Henry*), Grace Arnold (*Aunt Helen*), George Woodbridge (*Mr. Kemp*), Nora Gordon (*Mrs. Kemp*), David Grahame (*Poacher*), Jeanne of Bothkennar (*Dan, the dog*).

The Abominable Snowman (1957)
[USA: **The Abominable Snowman of the Himalayas**]
Dir: Val Guest. *Sc:* Nigel Kneale, from his TV play. *Ph:* Arthur Grant. *Prod. des:* Bernard Robinson. *Art dir:* Ted Marshall. *Ed:* Bill Lenny. *Mus:* John Hollingsworth. *Exec. prod:* Michael Carreras. *Prod:* Aubrey Baring. *Rel:* Warner Bros. (Britain), 20th Century-Fox (USA). 91 mins (Britain), 85 mins (USA). RegalScope.
With Forrest Tucker (*Tom Friend*), Peter Cushing (*Dr. John Rollason*), Maureen Connell (*Helen Rollason*), Richard Wattis (*Peter Fox*), Robert Brown (*Ed Shelley*), Michael Brill (*McNee*), Wolfe Morris (*Kusang*), Arnold Marle (*Lhama*), Anthony Chin.

Danger List (1957)
An Exclusive Production
Dir: Leslie Arliss. *Sc:* J. D. Scott. *Ph:* Arthur Grant. *Art dir:* Ted Marshall. *Ed:* James Needs, A. E. Cox. *Prod:* Anthony Hinds. *Rel:* Exclusive. 22 mins.
With Philip Friend (*Dr. Jim Bennett*), Honor Blackman (*Gillian Freeman*), Mervyn Johns (*Mr. Ellis*), Constance Fraser (*Mrs. Ellis*).

Clean Sweep (1958)
Dir: Maclean Rogers. *Ph:* Arthur Grant. *Art dir:* Ted Marshall. *Ed:* James Needs, A. E. Cox. *Assoc. prod:* Anthony Nelson-Keys. *Exec. prod:* Michael Carreras. *Prod:* Anthony Hinds. 29 mins.
With Eric Barker (*George Watson*), Thora Hird (*Vera Watson*), Vera Day (*Beryl Watson*), Ian Whittaker (*Dick Watson*), Wallas Eaton (*Ted*), Bill Fraser (*Bookmaker*).

The Camp on Blood Island (1958)
Dir: Val Guest. *Sc:* Jon Manchip White, Val Guest, from a story by Jon Manchip White. *Ph:* Jack Asher. *Art dir:* John Stoll. *Ed:* James Needs, Bill Lenny. *Mus:* Gerard Schurmann. *Exec. prod:* Michael Carreras. *Prod:* Anthony Hinds. *Rel:* Columbia. 82 mins. MegaScope.

With Andre Morell (*Colonel Lambert*), Carl Mohner (*Piet Van Elst*), Edward Underdown (*Major Dawes*), Walter Fitzgerald (*Cyril Beattie*), Phil Brown (*Lt. Bellamy*), Barbara Shelley (*Kate Keiller*), Michael Goodliffe (*Father Anjou*), Michael Gwynn (*Tom Shields*), Richard Wordsworth (*Dr. Keiller*), Ronald Radd (*Colonel Yamamitsu*).

Dracula (1958)
[USA: **Horror of Dracula**]
Dir: Terence Fisher. *Sc:* Jimmy Sangster, from the novel by Bram Stoker. *Ph:* Jack Asher. *Art dir:* Bernard Robinson. *Ed:* James Needs, Bill Lenny. *Mus:* James Bernard. *Prod:* Anthony Hinds. *Rel:* Universal (Britain: through Rank). 82 mins. Eastman Colour.
With Peter Cushing (*Dr. Van Helsing*), Christopher Lee (*Count Dracula*), Michael Gough (*Arthur*), Melissa Stribling (*Mina*), Carol Marsh (*Lucy*), Olga Dickie (*Gerda*), John Van Eyssen (*Jonathan Harker*), Valerie Gaunt (*Vampire Woman*).

The Snorkel (1958)
Dir: Guy Green. *Sc:* Peter Myers, Jimmy Sangster, from a story by Anthony Dawson. *Ph:* Jack Asher. *Art dir:* John Stoll. *Ed:* James Needs, Bill Lenny. *Prod:* Michael Carreras. *Rel:* Columbia. 90 mins (Britain), 74 mins (USA).
With Peter Van Eyck (*Jacques Duval*), Betta St. John (*Jean*), Mandy Miller (*Candy*), Gregoire Aslan (*The Inspector*), William Franklyn (*Wilson*).

Further Up the Creek (1958)
A Byron—Hammer Production
Dir: Val Guest. *Sc:* Val Guest, John Warren, Len Heath. *Ph:* Gerry Gibbs. *Art dir:* George Provis. *Ed:* Bill Lenny. *Mus:* Stanley Black. *Prod:* Henry Halsted. *Rel:* Columbia. 91 mins. MegaScope.
With David Tomlinson (*Lt. Fairweather*), Frankie Howerd (*Bosun*), Shirley Eaton (*Jane*), Thora Hird (*Mrs. Galloway*), Eric Pohlmann (*President*), Lionel Jeffries (*Barker*).
(This film was a sequel to *Up the Creek* which, though made in HammerScope and released by Exclusive, is on record as solely a Byron production.)

Man with a Dog (1958)
Dir: Leslie Arliss. *Ph:* Arthur Grant. *Art dir:* Ted Marshall. *Ed:* James Needs, A. E. Cox. *Assoc. prod:* Anthony Nelson-Keys. *Exec. prod:* Michael Carreras. *Prod:* Anthony Hinds. *Rel:* Exclusive 20 mins.
With Maurice Denham (*Mr. Keeble*), Sarah Lawson (*Vicky Alexandra*), Clifford Evans (*Dr. Bennett*), John van Eyssen (*D. Langham*), Marianne Stone (*Mrs. Stephens*).

The Revenge of Frankenstein (1958)
Dir: Terence Fisher. *Sc:* Jimmy Sangster, with

additional dialogue by H. Hurford Janes. *Ph:* Jack
Asher. *Prod. des:* Bernard Robinson. *Ed:* James
Needs, Alfred Cox. *Mus:* Leonard Salzedo. *Assoc.
prod:* Anthony Nelson-Keys. *Exec prod:* Michael
Carreras. *Prod:* Anthony Hinds. *Rel:* Columbia.
89 mins. Technicolor.
With Peter Cushing (*Dr. Victor Stein*), Francis
Matthews (*Dr. Hans Kleve*), Eunice Gayson
(*Margaret*), Michael Gwynn (*Karl*), John Welsh
(*Bergman*), Lionel Jeffries (*Fritz*).

I Only Arsked (1959)
A Hammer—Granada Production
Dir: Montgomery Tully. *Sc:* Sid Colin, Jack Davies,
from the Granada TV series "The Army Game".
Ph: Lionel Banes. *Art dir:* John Stoll. *Ed:* James
Needs, Alfred Cox. *Mus:* Benjamin Frankel. *Assoc
prod:* Anthony Nelson-Keys. *Exec. prod:* Michael
Carreras. *Prod:* Anthony Hinds. *Rel:* Columbia.
82 mins.
With Bernard Bresslaw (*Popeye*), Michael Medwin
(*Corporal Springer*), Alfie Bass (*Excused Boots*),
Geoffrey Summer (*Major Upshot-Bagley*), Charles
Hawtrey (*The Professor*), Norman Rossington
(*Cupcake*), David Lodge (*Sergeant "Potty"
Chambers*).

The Hound of the Baskervilles (1959)
Dir: Terence Fisher: *Sc:* Peter Bryan, from the
novel by Sir Arthur Conan Doyle. *Ph:* Jack Asher.
Art dir: Bernard Robinson. *Ed:* James Needs. *Mus:*
James Bernard. *Exec. prod:* Michael Carreras.
Assoc. prod: Anthony Nelson-Keys. *Prod:*
Anthony Hinds. *Rel:* United Artists. 87 mins.
Technicolor.
With Peter Cushing (*Sherlock Holmes*), Andre
Morell (*Dr. Watson*), Christopher Lee (*Sir Henry*),
Marla Landi (*Cecile*), Ewen Solon (*Stapleton*),
Francis De Wolff (*Dr. Mortimer*), Miles Malleson
(*Bishop Frankland*), John Le Mesurier (*Barry-
more*), David Oxley (*Sir Hugo Baskerville*).

Ten Seconds to Hell (1959)
A Hammer—Seven Arts Production
Dir: Robert Aldrich. *Sc:* Robert Aldrich, Teddi
Sherman, from the novel *The Phoenix* by
Lawrence P. Bachmann. *Ph:* Ernest Laszlo. *Art dir:*
Ken Adam. *Ed:* James Needs, Henry Richardson.
Mus: Kenneth V. Jones. *Prod:* Michael Carreras.
Rel: United Artists. 94 mins.
With Jack Palance (*Eric Koertner*), Jeff Chandler
(*Karl Wirtz*), Martine Carol (*Margot Hofer*), Robert
Cornthwaite (*Loeffler*), Dave Willock (*Tillig*), Wes
Addy (*Sulke*).

The Ugly Duckling (1959)
Dir: Lance Comfort. *Sc:* Sid Colin, Jack Davies,
from a story by Sid Colin. *Ph:* Michael Reed. *Art
dir:* Bernard Robinson. *Ed:* James Needs, John
Dunsford. *Mus:* Douglas Gamley. *Assoc. prod:*
Tommy Lyndon-Haynes. *Exec. prod:* Michael
Carreras. *Rel:* Columbia. 84 mins.
With Bernard Bresslaw (*Henry Jekyll/Teddy*

Hyde), Reginald Beckwith (*Reginald*), Jon Pertwee
(*Victor Jekyll*), Maudie Edwards (*Henrietta
Jekyll*).

Operation Universe (1959)
Dir: Peter Bryan. *Sc:* Peter Bryan. *Ph:* Len Harris.
Ed: Bill Lenny. *Prod:* Peter Bryan. *Rel:* Columbia.
28 mins. Technicolor. HammerScope.
With Robert Beatty (*Narrator*).
(Documentary.)

Yesterday's Enemy (1959)
Dir: Val Guest. *Sc:* Peter R. Newman, from his TV
play. *Ph:* Arthur Grant. *Art dir:* Bernard Robinson,
Don Mingave. *Ed:* James Needs, Alfred Cox. *Exec
prod:* Michael Carreras. *Rel:* Columbia. 95 mins.
MegaScope.
With Stanley Baker (*Captain Langford*), Guy Rolfe
(*Padre*), Leo McKern (*Max*), Gordon Jackson (*Sgt.
MacKenzie*), David Oxley (*Doctor*), Richard Pasco
(*2nd Lt. Hastings*), Russell Waters (*Brigadier*),
Philip Ahn (*Yamazaki*), Bryan Forbes (*Dawson*).

The Mummy (1959)
Dir: Terence Fisher. *Sc:* Jimmy Sangster, from the
screenplay of *The Mummy* (1932) by John L.
Balderston based on a story by Nina Wilcox
Putnam and Richard Schayer. *Ph:* Jack Asher. *Art
dir:* Bernard Robinson. *Ed:* James Needs, Alfred
Cox. *Mus:* Frank Reizenstein. *Assoc. prod:*
Anthony Nelson-Keys. *Prod:* Michael Carreras.
Rel: Universal (Britain: through Rank). 88 mins.
Technicolor.
With Peter Cushing (*John Banning*), Christopher
Lee (*Kharis*), Yvonne Furneaux (*Isobel/Ananka*),
Felix Aylmer (*Stephen Banning*), Eddie Byrne
(*Mulrooney*), Raymond Huntley (*Joseph
Whemple*), George Pastell (*Mehemet*).

The Man who could Cheat Death (1959)
Dir: Terence Fisher. *Sc:* Jimmy Sangster, from the
play *The Man in Half Moon Street* by Barré
Lyndon. *Ph:* Jack Asher. *Art dir:* Bernard
Robinson. *Ed:* James Needs. *Mus:* John
Hollingsworth. *Exec. prod:* Michael Carreras.
Assoc. prod: Anthony Nelson-Keys. *Prod:*
Anthony Hinds. *Rel:* Paramount. 83 mins. Techni-
color.
With Anton Diffring (*Doctor Georges Bonner*),
Hazel Court (*Janine*), Christopher Lee (*Pierre*),
Arnold Marle (*Ludwig*), Delphi Lawrence (*Margo*),
Francis De Wolff (*Legris*).

Don't Panic Chaps! (1959)
A Hammer—A.C.T. Production
Dir: George Pollock. *Sc:* Jack Davies, from a story
by Michael Corston and Ronald Holroyd. *Ph:*
Arthur Graham. *Art dir:* Scott MacGregor. *Ed:*
Harry Aldous. *Mus:* Philip Green. *Exec. prod:*
Ralph Bond. *Prod:* Teddy Baird. *Rel:* Columbia.
85 mins.
With Dennis Price (*Krisling*), George Cole (*Finch*),

Thorley Walters (*Brown*), Harry Fowler (*Ackroyd*), Nadja Regin (*Elsa*), Nicholas Phipps (*Mortimer*), Percy Herbert (*Bolter*).

The Stranglers of Bombay (1960)

Dir: Terence Fisher. *Sc:* David Z. Goodman. *Ph:* Arthur Grant. *Art dir:* Bernard Robinson, Don Mingaye. *Ed:* James Needs, Alfred Cox. *Mus:* James Bernard. *Assoc. prod:* Anthony Nelson-Keys. *Exec. prod:* Michael Carreras. *Prod:* Anthony Hinds. *Rel:* Columbia. 80 mins. MegaScope.
With Guy Rolfe (*Captain Lewis*), Allan Cuthbertson (*Captain Connaught-Smith*), Andrew Cruickshank (*Henderson*), Marne Maitland (*Patel Shari*), George Pastell (*High Priest*).

Hell is a City (1960)

Dir: Val Guest. *Sc:* Val Guest, from a novel by Maurice Proctor. *Ph:* Arthur Grant. *Art dir:* Robert Jones. *Ed:* James Needs, John Dunsford. *Mus:* Stanley Black. *Prod:* Michael Carreras. *Rel:* Associated British through Warner-Pathe. 98 mins. HammerScope.
With Stanley Baker (*Inspector Martineau*), John Crawford (*Don Starling*), Donald Pleasence (*Gus Hawkins*), Maxine Audley (*Julia Martineau*), Billie Whitelaw (*Chloe Hawkins*).

The Curse of the Werewolf (1960)

A Hammer–Hotspur Production
Dir: Terence Fisher. *Sc:* John Elder [Anthony Hinds], from the novel *The Werewolf of Paris* by Guy Endore. *Ph:* Arthur Grant. *Art dir:* Bernard Robinson, Thomas Goswell. *Ed:* James Needs, Alfred Cox. *Mus:* Benjamin Frankel. *Assoc. prod:* Anthony Nelson-Keys. *Exec. prod:* Michael Carreras. *Prod:* Anthony Hinds. *Rel:* Universal (Britain: through Rank). 88 mins. Technicolor.
With Oliver Reed (*Léon*), Clifford Evans (*Don Alfredo Carido*), Hira Talfrey (*Teresa*), Catherine Feller (*Cristina*), Yvonne Romain (*Jailer's daughter*), Anthony Dawson (*Marques*), Richard Wordsworth (*Beggar*), Warren Mitchell (*Pepe Valiente*).

The Brides of Dracula (1960)

A Hammer–Hotspur Production
Dir: Terence Fisher. *Sc:* Jimmy Sangster, Peter Bryan, Edward Percy. *Ph:* Jack Asher. *Art dir:* Bernard Robinson, Thomas Goswell. *Ed:* Jim Needs, Alfred Cox. *Mus:* Malcolm Williamson. *Assoc. prod:* Anthony Nelson-Keys. *Exec prod:* Michael Carreras. *Prod:* Anthony Hinds. *Rel:* Universal (Britain: through Rank). 85 mins. Technicolor.
With Peter Cushing (*Van Helsing*), Yvonne Monlaur (*Marianne*), Freda Jackson (*Greta*), David Peel (*Baron Meinster*), Martita Hunt (*Baroness Meinster*), Andree Melly (*Gina*), Mona Washbourne (*Frau Lang*), Henry Oscar (*Lang*).

Never Take Sweets from a Stranger (1960)

Dir: Cyril Frankel. *Sc:* John Hunter, from the play *The Pony Cart* by Roger Garis. *Ph:* Freddie Francis. *Art dir:* Bernard Robinson, Don Mingaye. *Ed:* Jim Needs, Alfred Cox. *Mus:* Elisabeth Lutyens. *Assoc. prod:* Anthony Nelson-Keys. *Exec. prod:* Michael Carreras. *Prod:* Anthony Hinds. *Rel:* Columbia. 81 mins. MegaScope.
With Gwen Watford (*Sally*), Patrick Allen (*Peter Carter*), Felix Aylmer (*Olderberry Sr.*), Niall MacGinnis (*Defence Counsel*), Alison Leggatt (*Martha*), Bill Nagy (*Olderberry Jr.*).

The Two Faces of Dr. Jekyll (1960)
[USA: House of Fright]

Dir: Terence Fisher. *Sc:* Wolf Mankowitz, from the novel *The Strange Case of Dr Jekyll and Mr Hyde* by Robert Louis Stevenson. *Ph:* Jack Asher. *Art dir:* Bernard Robinson. *Ed:* Jim Needs, Eric Boyd-Perkins. *Mus:* Monty Norman, David Heneker. *Assoc prod:* Anthony Nelson-Keys. *Prod:* Michael Carreras. *Rel:* Columbia (Britain), American International (USA). 88 mins. Technicolor. MegaScope.
With Paul Massie (*Jekyll/Hyde*), Dawn Addams (*Kitty Jekyll*), Christopher Lee (*Paul Allen*), David Kossoff (*Litauer*), Francis De Wolff (*Inspector*).

Sword of Sherwood Forest (1960)

A Hammer–Yeoman Production
Dir: Terence Fisher. *Sc:* Alan Hackney. *Ph:* Ken Hodges. *Art dir:* John Stoll. *Ed:* James Needs, Lee Doig. *Mus:* Alun Hoddinott. *Exec. prod:* Michael Carreras. *Prod:* Richard Greene, Sidney Cole. *Rel:* Columbia. 80 mins. Technicolor. MegaScope.
With Richard Green (*Robin Hood*), Peter Cushing (*Sheriff of Nottingham*), Richard Pasco (*Earl of Newark*), Niall MacGinnis (*Friar Tuck*), Jack Gwillim (*Hubert Walter, Archbishop of Canterbury*), Sarah Branch (*Maid Marion*), Nigel Green (*Little John*), Oliver Reed (*Melton*).

Visa to Canton (1961)
[USA: Passport to China]

A Hammer–Swallow Production
Dir: Michael Carreras. *Sc:* Gordon Wellesley. *Ph:* Arthur Grant. *Art dir:* Bernard Robinson, Thomas Goswell. *Ed:* James Needs, Alfred Cox. *Mus:* Edwin Astley. *Assoc. prod:* Anthony Nelson-Keys. *Prod:* Michael Carreras. *Rel:* Columbia. 75 mins. Technicolor.
With Richard Basehart (*Don Benton*), Lisa Gastoni (*Lola Sanchez*), Athene Seyler (*Mao Tai Tai*), Eric Pohlmann (*Ivano Kang*), Alan Gifford (*Orme*), Bernard Cribbins (*Pereira*), Burt Kwouk (*Jimmy*), Marne Maitland (*Han Po*).

The Full Treatment (1961)
[USA: Stop Me Before I Kill]

A Hilary–Falcon* Production
Dir: Val Guest. *Sc:* Val Guest, Ronald Scott Thorn, from the novel by Ronald Scott Thorn. *Ph:* Gilbert Taylor. *Art dir:* Tony Masters. *Ed:* Bill Lenny. *Mus:* Stanley Black. *Assoc. prod:* Victor

Lyndon. *Prod:* Val Guest. *Rel:* Columbia. 109 mins. MegaScope.
With Claude Dauphin (*David Prade*), Diane Cilento (*Denise Colby*), Ronald Lewis (*Alan Colby*), Francoise Rosay (*Mrs. Prade*), Bernard Braden (*Stoneyhouse*), Katya Douglas (*Connie*).
*Falcon was a subsidiary of Hammer.

A Weekend with Lulu (1961)
Dir: John Paddy Carstairs. *Sc:* Ted Lloyd, from a story by Ted Lloyd and Val Valentine. *Ph:* Ken Hodges. *Art dir:* John Howell. *Ed:* James Needs, Tom Simpson. *Mus:* Trevor H. Stanford. *Exec. prod:* Michael Carreras. *Prod:* Ted Lloyd. *Rel:* Columbia. 89 mins.
With Bob Monkhouse (*Fred*), Leslie Phillips (*Tim*), Alfred Marks (*Comte de Grenoble*), Shirley Eaton (*Deirdre*), Irene Handl (*Florence Proudfoot*), Sidney James (*Cafe Patron*), Kenneth Connor (*British tourist*).

Taste of Fear (1961)
[USA: **Scream of Fear**]
Dir: Seth Holt. *Sc:* Jimmy Sangster. *Ph:* Douglas Slocombe. *Prod. des:* Bernard Robinson. *Art dir:* Tom Goswell. *Ed:* James Needs, Eric Boyd Perkins. *Mus:* Clifton Parker. *Exec. prod:* Michael Carreras. *Prod:* Jimmy Sangster. *Rel:* Columbia. 82 mins.
With Susan Strasberg (*Penny Appleby*), Ronald Lewis (*Bob*), Ann Todd (*Jane Appleby*), Christopher Lee (*Dr. Gerrard*), Leonard Sachs, Anne Blake, John Serret, Fred Johnson.

Watch it Sailor! (1961)
Dir: Wolf Rilla. *Sc:* Falkland Cary, Philip King, from their stage play. *Ph:* Arthur Grant. *Art dir:* Bernard Robinson, Don Mingaye. *Ed:* James Needs, Alfred Cox. *Mus:* Douglas Gamley. *Assoc. prod:* Anthony Nelson-keys. *Exec. prod:* Michael Carreras. *Prod:* Maurice Cowan. *Rel:* Columbia (Britain: through BLC). 81 mins.
With Dennis Price (*Lt.-Cmdr. Hardcastle*), Liz Fraser (*Daphne*), Irene Handl (*Edie Hornett*), Graham Stark (*Carnoustie Bligh*), Vera Day (*Shirley Hornett*).

The Terror of the Tongs (1961)
A Hammer—Merlin Production
Dir: Anthony Bushell. *Sc:* Jimmy Sangster. *Ph:* Arthur Grant. *Art dir:* Bernard Robinson, Thomas Goswell. *Ed:* Jim Needs, Eric Boyd-Perkins. *Mus:* James Bernard. *Assoc. prod:* Anthony Nelson-Keys. *Exec. prod:* Michael Carreras. *Prod:* Kenneth Hyman. *Rel:* Columbia (Britain: through BLC). 79 mins. Technicolor.
With Geoffrey Toone (*Jackson*), Christopher Lee (*Chung King*), Yvonne Monlaur (*Lee*), Brian Worth (*Harcourt*), Richard Leech (*Inspector Dean*).

The Phantom of the Opera (1962)
Dir: Terence Fisher. *Sc:* John Elder [Anthony

Hinds], from the story by Gaston Leroux. *Ph:* Arthur Grant. *Art dir:* Bernard Robinson, Don Mingaye. *Ed:* James Needs, Alfred Cox. *Mus:* Edwin Astley. *Assoc. prod:* Basil Keys. *Prod:* Anthony Hinds. *Rel:* Universal (Britain: through Rank). 84 mins. Technicolor.
With Herbert Lom (*The Phantom*), Edward De Souza (*Harry Hunter*), Heather Sears (*Christine Charles*), Michael Gough (*Lord Ambrose D'Arcy*), Thorley Walters (*Lattimer*), Ian Wilson (*Dwarf*).

Captain Clegg (1962)
[USA: **Night Creatures**]
A Hammer—Major Production
Dir: Peter Graham Scott. *Sc:* John Elder [Anthony Hinds], with additional dialogue by Barbara S. Harper. *Ph:* Arthur Grant. *Art dir:* Bernard Robinson, Don Mingaye. *Ed:* James Needs, Eric Boyd-Perkins. *Mus:* Don Banks. *Prod:* John Temple-Smith. *Rel:* Universal (Britain: through Rank). 82 mins. Technicolor.
With Peter Cushing (*Dr. Blyss, alias Captain Clegg*), Patrick Allen (*Captain Collier*), Oliver Reed (*Harry*), Michael Ripper (*Mipps*), Derek Francis (*Squire*).

The Pirates of Blood River (1962)
Dir: John Gilling. *Sc:* John Hunter, John Gilling, from a story by Jimmy Sangster. *Ph:* Arthur Grant. *Art dir:* Bernard Robinson, Don Mingaye. *Ed:* James Needs, Eric Boyd-Perkins. *Exec. prod:* Michael Carreras. *Prod:* Anthony Nelson-Keys. *Rel:* Columbia (Britain: through BLC). 84 mins. Colour. HammerScope.
With Kerwin Mathews (*Jonathon Standing*), Glenn Corbett (*Henry*), Christopher Lee (*La Roche*), Marla Landi (*Bess*), Oliver Reed (*Brocaire*), Andrew Keir (*Jason Standing*), Peter Arne (*Hench*).

Maniac (1963)
Dir: Michael Carreras. *Sc:* Jimmy Sangster. *Ph:* Wilkie Cooper. *Art dir:* Edward Carrick. *Ed:* James Needs, Tom Simpson. *Prod:* Jimmy Sangster. *Rel:* Columbia (Britain: through BLC). 86 mins.
With Kerwin Mathews (*Geoff Farrell*), Nadia Gray (*Eve*), Donald Houston (*Georges*), Liliane Brousse (*Annette*).

The Damned (1963)
[USA: **These Are the Damned**]
A Hammer—Swallow Production
Dir: Joseph Losey. *Sc:* Evan Jones, from the novel *The Children of Light* by H. L. Lawrence. *Ph:* Arthur Grant. *Prod. des:* Bernard Robinson. *Art dir:* Don Mingaye. *Ed:* James Needs, Reginald Mills. *Mus:* James Bernard. *Assoc. prod:* Anthony Nelson-Keys. *Exec. prod:* Michael Carreras. *Prod:* Anthony Hinds. *Rel:* Columbia (Britain: through BLC) (USA, in 1965). 87 mins (Britain), 77 mins (USA). HammerScope.

With Macdonald Carey (*Simon Wells*), Shirley Ann Field (*Joan*), Viveca Lindfors (*Freya Neilson*), Alexander Knox (*Bernard*), Oliver Reed (*King*).

The Scarlet Blade (1963)
[USA: **The Crimson Blade**]
Dir: John Gilling. *Sc:* John Gilling. *Ph:* Jack Asher. *Prod. des:* Bernard Robinson. *Art dir:* Don Mingaye. *Ed:* John Dunsford. *Mus:* Gary Hughes. *Prod:* Anthony Nelson-Keys. *Rel:* Warner-Pathe (Britain), Columbia (USA). 82 mins. Technicolor. HammerScope.
With Lionel Jeffries (*Colonel Judd*), Oliver Reed (*Sylvester*), Jack Hedley (*Edward Beverly*), June Thorburn (*Clare*), Duncan Lamont (*Major Bell*), Suzan Farmer (*Constance*).

Cash on Demand (1963)
A Woodpecker–Hammer Production
Dir: Quentin Lawrence. *Sc:* David T. Chantler, Lewis Greifer, from the TV play *The Gold Inside* by Jacques Gillies. *Ph:* Arthur Grant. *Art dir:* Don Mingaye. *Ed:* James Needs. *Mus:* Wilfred Josephs. *Prod:* Michael Carreras. *Rel:* Columbia (Britain: through BLC) (USA, in 1961). 66 mins.
With Peter Cushing (*Fordyce*), Andre Morell (*Hepburn*), Richard Vernon (*Pearson*), Barry Lowe (*Harvill*), Norman Bird (*Sanderson*).

Paranoiac (1963)
Dir: Freddie Francis. *Sc:* Jimmy Sangster. *Ph:* Arthur Grant. *Art dir:* Bernard Robinson, Don Mingaye. *Ed:* James Needs. *Mus:* Elisabeth Lutyens. *Assoc. prod:* Basil Keys. *Prod:* Anthony Hinds. *Rel:* Universal (Britain: through Rank). 80 mins.
With Janette Scott (*Eleanor*), Oliver Reed (*Simon*), Alexander Davion (*Tony*), Sheila Burrell (*Harriet*), Liliane Brousse (*Francoise*), Maurice Denham (*John Kossett*).

Kiss of the Vampire (1964)
Dir: Don Sharp. *Sc:* John Elder [Anthony Hinds]. *Ph:* Alan Hume. *Prod. des:* Bernard Robinson. *Art dir:* Don Mingaye. *Ed:* James Needs. *Mus:* James Bernard. *Prod:* Anthony Hinds. *Rel:* Universal (Britain: through Rank). 87 mins. Eastman Colour.
With Clifford Evans (*Prof. Zimmer*), Noel Willman (*Ravna*), Edward de Souza (*Gerald Harcourt*), Jennifer Daniel (*Marianne*).

The Evil of Frankenstein (1964)
Dir: Freddie Francis. *Sc:* John Elder [Anthony Hinds]. *Ph:* John Wilcox. *Art dir:* Don Mingaye. *Ed:* James Needs. *Mus:* Don Banks. *Prod:* Anthony Hinds. *Rel:* Universal (Britain: through Rank). 84 mins. Eastman Colour.
With Peter Cushing (*Baron Frankenstein*), Peter Woodthorpe (*Zoltan*), Sandor Eles (*Hans*), Kiwi Kingston (*The Creature*), Duncan Lamont (*Chief of Police*).

Nightmare (1964)
Dir: Freddie Francis. *Sc:* Jimmy Sangster. *Ph:* John Wilcox. *Art dir:* Bernard Robinson, Don Mingaye. *Ed:* James Needs. *Mus:* Don Banks. *Prod:* Jimmy Sangster. *Rel:* Universal (Britain: through Rank). 82 mins. HammerScope.
With David Knight (*Henry Baxter*), Moira Redmond (*Grace Maddox*), Jennie Linden (*Janet*), Brenda Bruce (*Mary Lewis*), George A. Cooper (*John*), Irene Richmond (*Mrs. Gibbs*).

The Devil-Ship Pirates (1964)
Dir: Don Sharp. *Sc:* Jimmy Sangster. *Ph:* Michael Reed. *Art dir:* Bernard Robinson, Don Mingaye. *Ed:* James Needs. *Mus:* Gary Hughes. *Prod:* Anthony Nelson-Keys. *Rel:* Associated British-Pathe (Britain), Columbia (USA, 1963). 86 mins. Technicolor. HammerScope.
With Christopher Lee (*Captain Robeles*), John Cairney (*Harry*), Barry Warren (*Manuel*), Ernest Clark (*Sir Basil Smeeton*).

The Gorgon (1964)
Dir: Terence Fisher. *Sc:* John Gilling, from a story by J. Llewellyn Devine. *Ph:* Michael Reed. *Art dir:* Bernard Robinson, Don Mingaye. *Ed:* James Needs, Eric Boyd Perkins. *Mus:* James Bernard. *Prod:* Anthony Nelson-Keys. *Rel:* Columbia (Britain: through BLC). 83 mins. Technicolor.
With Peter Cushing (*Namaroff*), Richard Pasco (*Paul*), Barbara Shelley (*Carla Hoffman*), Christopher Lee (*Professor Meister*), Michael Goodliffe (*Prof. Heitz*), Patrick Troughton (*Kanof*), Jack Watson (*Ratoff*).

The Curse of the Mummy's Tomb (1964)
A Hammer–Swallow Production
Dir: Michael Carreras. *Sc:* Henry Younger [Michael Carreras]. *Ph:* Otto Heller. *Art dir:* Bernard Robinson. *Ed:* James Needs, Eric Boyd Perkins. *Mus:* Carlo Martelli. *Assoc. prod:* Bill Hill. *Prod:* Michael Carreras. *Rel:* Columbia (Britain: through BLC). 80 mins. Technicolor. Techniscope.
With Terence Morgan (*Adam Beauchamp*), Fred Clark (*Alexander King*), Ronald Howard (*John Bray*), Jeanne Roland (*Annette Dubois*), George Pastell (*Hashmi Bey*), Jack Gwillim (*Sir Giles Dalrymple*).

Fanatic (1965)
[USA: **Die! Die! My Darling!**]
A Hammer–Seven Arts Production
Dir: Silvio Narizzano. *Sc:* Richard Matheson, from the novel *Nightmare* by Anne Blaisdell. *Ph:* Arthur Ibbetson. *Prod. des:* Peter Proud. *Ed:* James Needs, John Dunsford. *Mus:* Wilfred Josephs. *Exec. prod:* Michael Carreras. *Prod:* Anthony Hinds. *Rel:* Columbia (Britain: through BLC). 96 mins (Britain), 105 mins (USA). Technicolor.
With Tallulah Bankhead (*Mrs. Trefoile*), Stefanie Powers (*Patricia Carroll*), Peter Vaughan (*Harry*), Maurice Kaufman (*Alan*), Yootha Joyce (*Anna*), Donald Sutherland (*Joseph*).

She (1965)
Dir: Robert Day. *Sc:* David T. Chantler, from the novel by H. Rider Haggard. *Ph:* Harry Waxman. *Art dir:* Robert Jones, Don Mingaye. *Ed:* James Needs, Eric Boyd-Perkins. *Mus:* James Bernard. *Assoc. prod:* Aida Young. *Prod:* Michael Carreras. *Rel:* Associated British (Britain, through Warner-Pathe), Metro-Goldwyn-Mayer (USA). 105 mins. Technicolor. HammerScope.
With John Richardson (*Leo Vincey*), Ursula Andress (*Ayesha*), Peter Cushing (*Major Holly*), Bernard Cribbins (*Job*), Rosenda Monteros (*Ustane*), Christopher Lee (*Billali*), Andre Morell (*Haumeid*), John Maxim.

The Secret of Blood Island (1965)
Dir: Quentin Lawrence. *Sc:* John Gilling. *Ph:* Jack Asher. *Prod. des:* Bernard Robinson. *Ed:* James Needs, Tom Simpson. *Mus:* James Bernard. *Prod:* Anthony Nelson-Keys. *Rel:* Universal (Britain: through Rank). 84 mins. Eastman Colour.
With Barbara Shelley (*Elaine*), Jack Hedley (*Sgt. Crewe*), Charles Tingwell (*Major Dryden*), Bill Owen (*Bludgin*).

Hysteria (1965)
Dir: Freddie Francis. *Sc:* Jimmy Sangster. *Ph:* John Wilcox. *Prod. des:* Edward Carrick. *Ed:* James Needs. *Mus:* Don Banks. *Prod:* Jimmy Sangster. *Rel:* Metro-Goldwyn-Mayer. 85 mins.
With Robert Webber (*Mr. Smith*), Lelia Goldoni (*Denise*), Anthony Newlands (*Doctor Keller*), Jennifer Jayne (*Gina*), Maurice Denham (*Hemmings*), Peter Woodthorpe, Sandra Boize, Sue Lloyd.

The Brigand of Kandahar (1965)
Dir: John Gilling. *Sc:* John Gilling. *Ph:* Reg Wyer. *Prod. des:* Bernard Robinson. *Art dir:* Don Mingaye. *Ed:* James Needs, Tom Simpson. *Mus:* Don Banks. *Prod:* Anthony Nelson-Keys. *Rel:* Warner-Pathe (Britain), Columbia (USA). 81 mins. Technicolor. 'Scope.
With Ronald Lewis (*Lt. Case*), Oliver Reed (*Eli Khan*), Duncan Lamont (*Col. Drewe*), Yvonne Romain (*Ratina*).

The Nanny (1965)
A Hammer—Seven Art Production
Dir: Seth Holt. *Sc:* Jimmy Sangster, from the novel by Evelyn Piper. *Ph:* Harry Waxman. *Prod. des:* Edward Carrick. *Ed:* James Needs, Tom Simpson. *Mus:* Richard Rodney Bennett. *Exec. prod:* Anthony Hinds. *Prod:* Jimmy Sangster. *Rel:* Associated British (Britain, through Warner-Pathe), 20th Century-Fox (USA). 93 mins.
With Bette Davis (*The Nanny*), Wendy Craig (*Virginia Fane*), Jill Bennett (*Penelope Fane*), James Villiers (*Bill Fane*), William Dix (*Joey Fane*), Pamela Franklin (*Bobby*), Jack Watling (*Dr. Medman*), Maurice Denham (*Dr. Beamaster*), Alfred Burke (*Dr. Wills*).

Dracula — Prince of Darkness (1966)
A Hammer—Seven Arts Production
Dir: Terence Fisher. *Sc:* John Sansom, from an idea by John Elder [Anthony Hinds] based on characters created by Bram Stoker. *Ph:* Michael Reed. *Prod. des:* Bernard Robinson. *Art dir:* Don Mingaye. *Ed:* James Needs, Chris Barnes. *Mus:* James Bernard. *Prod:* Anthony Nelson-Keys. *Rel:* Warner-Pathe (Britain), 20th Century-Fox (USA) 90 mins.
With Christopher Lee (*Dracula*), Barbara Shelley (*Helen*), Andrew Keir (*Father Sandor*), Francis Matthews (*Charles*), Suzan Farmer (*Diana*), Charles Tingwell (*Alan*), Thorley Walters (*Ludwig*).

The Plague of the Zombies (1966)
Dir: John Gilling. *Sc:* Peter Bryan. *Ph:* Arthur Grant. *Prod. des:* Bernard Robinson. *Art dir:* Don Mingaye. *Ed:* James Needs, Chris Barnes. *Mus:* James Bernard. *Prod:* Anthony Nelson-Keys. *Rel:* Warner-Pathe (Britain), 20th Century-Fox (USA). 91 mins. Technicolor.
With Andre Morell (*Sir James Forbes*), Diane Clare (*Sylvia*), Brook Williams (*Dr. Peter Tompson*), Jacqueline Pearce (*Alice*), John Carson (*Clive Hamilton*).

Rasputin — the Mad Monk (1966)
Dir: Don Sharp. *Sc:* John Elder [Anthony Hinds]. *Ph:* Michael Reed. *Prod. des:* Bernard Robinson. *Art dir:* Don Mingaye. *Ed:* James Needs, Roy Hyde. *Mus:* Don Banks. *Prod:* Anthony Nelson-Keys. *Rel:* Warner-Pathe (Britain), 20th Century-Fox (USA). 91 mins. Technicolor. CinemaScope.
With Christopher Lee (*Rasputin*), Barbara Shelley (*Sonia*), Richard Pasco (*Dr. Zargo*), Francis Matthews (*Ivan*).

The Reptile (1966)
Dir: John Gilling. *Sc:* John Elder [Anthony Hinds]. *Ph:* Arthur Grant. *Prod. des:* Bernard Robinson. *Art dir:* Don Mingaye. *Ed:* James Needs, Roy Hyde. *Mus:* Don Banks. *Prod:* Anthony Nelson-Keys. *Rel:* Warner-Pathe (Britain), 20th Century-Fox (USA). 91 mins. Technicolor.
With Noel Willman (*Dr. Franklyn*), Jennifer Daniel (*Valerie Spalding*), Ray Barrett (*Harry Spalding*), Jacqueline Pearce (*Anna Franklyn*), Michael Ripper (*Tom Bailey*).

The Old Dark House (1966)
A Hammer—Wiliam Castle Production
Dir: William Castle. *Sc:* Robert Dillon, from the novel *Benighted* by J. B. Priestley. *Ph:* Arthur Grant. *Prod. des:* Bernard Robinson. *Ed:* James Needs. *Mus:* Benjamin Frankel. *Assoc prod:* Dona Holloway. *Prod:* William Castle, Anthony Hinds. *Rel:* Columbia (Britain, through BLC) (USA in 1963). 77 mins (Britain), 86 mins (USA). Colour.
With Tom Poston (*Tom Penderel*), Robert Morley (*Roderick Femm*), Janette Scott (*Cecily Femm*), Joyce Grenfell (*Agatha Femm*), Mervyn Johns (*Potiphar Femm*), Fenella Fielding (*Morgana Femm*), Peter Bull (*Casper/Jasper*), Danny Green (*Morgan Femm*), John Harvey.

The Witches (1966)
[USA: **The Devil's Own**]
A Hammer—Seven Arts Production
Dir: Cyril Frankel. *Sc:* Nigel Kneale, from the
novel *The Devil's Own* by Peter Curtis. *Ph:* Arthur
Grant. *Prod. des:* Bernard Robinson. *Art dir:* Don
Mingaye. *Ed:* James Needs, Chris Barnes. *Mus:*
Richard Rodney Bennett. *Prod:* Anthony Nelson-
Keys. *Rel:* Warner-Pathe (Britain), 20th Century-
Fox (USA). 91 mins. Technicolor.
With Joan Fontaine (*Gwen Mayfield*), Kay Walsh
(*Stephanie Bax*), Alec McCowen (*Alan Bax*), Ingrid
Brett (*Linda*), Martin Stephens (*Ronnie Dowsett*),
Gwen Ffrangcon-Davies (*Granny Rigg*), Duncan
Lamont (*Bob Curd*), Leonard Rossiter (*Dr. Wallis*).

One Million Years B.C. (1966)
A Hammer—Seven Arts Production
Dir: Don Chaffey. *Sc:* Michael Carreras, from the
screenplay of *One Million B.C.* (1940) by Mickell
Novak, George Baker and Joseph Frickert. *Ph:*
Wilkie Cooper. *Visual effects:* Ray Harryhausen.
Art dir: Robert Jones. *Ed:* James Needs, Tom
Simpson. *Mus:* Mario Nascimbene. *Assoc. prod:*
Aida Young. *Prod:* Michael Carreras. *Rel:* Warner-
Pathe (Britain), 20th Century-Fox (USA).
100 mins. (Britain), 91 mins (USA).
With John Richardson (*Tumak*), Raquel Welch
(*Loana*), Percy Herbert (*Sakana*), Robert Brown
(*Akhoba*), Martine Beswick (*Nupondi*).

The Viking Queen (1967)
Dir: Don Chaffey. *Sc:* Clarke Reynolds, from a
story by John Temple-Smith. *Ph:* Stephen Dade.
Prod. des: George Provis. *Ed:* James Needs, Peter
Boita. *Mus:* Gary Hughes. *Prod:* John Temple-
Smith. *Rel:* Warner-Pathe (Britain), 20th Century-
Fox (USA). 91 mins. Technicolor.
With Don Murray (*Justinian*), Carita (*Salina*),
Donald Houston (*Maelgan*), Andrew Keir
(*Octavian*), Patrick Troughton (*Tristram*),
Adrienne Corri (*Beatrice*), Niall MacGinnis
(*Tiberion*), Wilfrid Lawson (*King Priam*).

Frankenstein Created Woman (1967)
A Hammer—Seven Arts Production
Dir: Terence Fisher. *Sc:* John Elder [Anthony
Hinds]. *Ph:* Arthur Grant. *Prod. des:* Bernard
Robinson. *Art dir:* Don Mingaye. *Ed:* James Needs,
Spencer Reeve. *Mus:* James Bernard. *Prod:*
Anthony Nelson-Keys. *Rel:* Warner-Pathe (Britain),
20th Century-Fox (USA). 86 mins. Technicolor.
With Peter Cushing (*Baron Frankenstein*), Susan
Denberg (*Christina*), Thorley Walters (*Dr. Hertz*),
Robert Morris (*Hans*), Duncan Lamont (*The
Prisoner*).

The Mummy's Shroud (1967)
Dir: John Gilling. *Sc:* John Gilling, from a story by
John Elder [Anthony Hinds]. *Ph:* Arthur Grant.
Prod. des: Bernard Robinson. *Art dir:* Don
Mingaye. *Ed:* James Needs, Chris Barnes. *Mus:* Don
Banks. *Prod:* Anthony Nelson-Keys. *Rel:* Warner-
Pathe (Britain), 20th Century-Fox (USA). 84 mins.
Technicolor.
With John Phillips (*Stanley Preston*), Andre Morell
(*Sir Basil Walden*), David Buck (*Paul Preston*),
Elizabeth Sellars (*Barbara Preston*), Maggie
Kimberley (*Claire*).

Quatermass and the Pit (1967)
[USA: **Five Million Years to Earth**]
A Hammer—Seven Arts Production
Dir: Roy Ward Baker. *Sc:* Nigel Kneale, from his
TV serial. *Ph:* Arthur Grant. *Prod. des:* Bernard
Robinson. *Art dir:* Ken Ryan. *Ed:* James Needs,
Spencer Reeve. *Mus:* Tristram Cary. *Prod:*
Anthony Nelson-Keys. *Rel:* Warner-Pathe (Britain),
20th Century-Fox (USA). 97 mins. Technicolor.
With James Donald (*Dr. Matthew Roney*), Andrew
Keir (*Professor Quatermass*), Barbara Shelley
(*Barbara Judd*), Julian Glover (*Colonel Breen*),
Duncan Lamont (*Sladden*).

A Challenge for Robin Hood (1967)
Dir: C. M. Pennington-Richards. *Sc:* Peter Bryan.
Ph: Arthur Grant. *Art dir:* Maurice Carter. *Ed:*
James Needs, Chris Barnes. *Mus:* Gary Hughes.
Prod: Clifford Parkes. *Rel:* Warner-Pathe (Britain).
96 mins. Technicolor.
With Barrie Ingham (*Robin*), James Hayter (*Friar
Tuck*), Leon Greene (*Little John*), Gay Hamilton
(*Maid Marian*), Peter Blythe (*Roger de Courtenay*),
Jenny Till ("*Lady Marian*"), John Arnatt (*Sheriff
of Nottingham*), Eric Flynn (*Alan-a-Dale*).

The Anniversary (1968)
Dir: Roy Ward Baker.* *Sc:* Jimmy Sangster, from
the play by Bill MacIlwraith. *Ph:* Harry Waxman.
Art dir: Reece Pemberton. *Ed:* James Needs, Peter
Weatherley. *Prod:* Jimmy Sangster. *Rel:* Warner-
Pathe (Britain), 20th Century-Fox (USA). 95 mins.
Technicolor.
With Bette Davis (*Mrs. Taggart*), Sheila Hancock
(*Karen Taggart*), Jack Hedley (*Terry Taggart*),
James Cossins (*Henry Taggart*), Elaine Taylor
(*Shirley Blair*), Christian Roberts (*Tom Taggart*),
Timothy Bateson (*Mr. Bird*), Arnold Diamond.
* Replacing Alvin Rakoff who commenced the
film's direction.

The Vengeance of She (1968)
Dir: Cliff Owen. *Sc:* Peter O'Donnell, from charac-
ters created by H. Rider Haggard in his novel *She*.
Ph: Wolfgang Suschitzky. *Prod. des:* Lionel Couch.
Ed: Raymond Poulton. *Mus:* Mario Nascimbene.
Prod: Aida Young. *Rel:* Warner-Pathe (Britain),
20th Century-Fox (USA). 101 mins. Technicolor.
With John Richardson (*Killikrates*), Olinka Berova
(*Carol*), Edward Judd (*Philip Smith*), Colin
Blakeley (*George Carter*), Derek Godfrey (*Men-
Hari*), Jill Melford (*Sheila Carter*), George Sewell
(*Harry Walker*), Andre Morell (*Kassim*), Noel
Willman (*Za-Tor*).

The Devil Rides Out (1968)
[USA: **The Devil's Bride**]
Dir: Terence Fisher. *Sc:* Richard Matheson, from
the novel *The Devil Rides Out* by Dennis Wheatley.
Ph: Arthur Grant. *Art dir:* Bernard Robinson. *Ed:*
James Needs, Spencer Reeve. *Mus:* James Bernard.
Prod: Anthony Nelson-Keys. *Rel:* Warner-Pathe
(Britain), 20th Century-Fox (USA). 95 mins.
Technicolor.
With Christopher Lee (*Duc de Richleau*), Charles
Gray (*Mocata*), Nike Arrighi (*Tanith*), Leon Greene
(*Rex van Ryn*), Patrick Mower (*Simon Aron*),
Gwen Ffrangcon-Davies (*Countess d'Urfe*).

Slave Girls (1968)
[USA: **Prehistoric Women**]
Dir: Michael Carreras. *Sc:* Henry Younger [Michael
Carreras]. *Ph:* Michael Reed. *Art dir:* Robert
Jones. *Ed:* Jim Needs, Roy Hyde. *Mus:* Carlo
Mantelli. *Assoc. prod:* Aida Young. *Exec. prod:*
Anthony Hinds. *Prod:* Michael Carreras. *Rel:*
Warner-Pathe (Britain), 20th Century-Fox (USA,
1967). 95 mins (USA), 74 mins (Britain).
Technicolor. CinemaScope.
With Martine Beswick (*Kari*), Edina Ronay (*Saria*),
Michael Latimer (*David Marchant*), Stephanie
Randall (*Amyak*), Carol White (*Gido*), Alexandra
Stevenson (*Luri*).

Dracula has Risen from the Grave (1968)
Dir: Freddie Francis. *Sc:* John Elder [Anthony
Hinds] from the character created by Bram Stoker.
Ph: Arthur Grant. *Art dir:* Bernard Robinson. *Ed:*
James Needs, Spencer Reeve. *Mus:* James Bernard.
Prod: Aida Young. *Rel:* Warner-Pathe (Britain),
Warner Bros.—Seven Arts (USA). 92 mins.
Technicolor.
With Christopher Lee (*Count Dracula*), Rupert
Davies (*Monsignor*), Veronica Carlson (*Maria*),
Barbara Ewing (*Zena*), Barry Andrews (*Paul*),
Ewan Hooper (*Priest*), Marion Mathie (*Anna*).

The Lost Continent (1968)
Dir: Michael Carreras. *Sc:* Michael Nash, from the
novel *Uncharted Seas* by Dennis Wheatley. *Ph:*
Paul Beeson. *Art dir:* Arthur Lawson. *Special
effects:* Cliff Richardson. *Ed:* James Needs, Chris
Barnes. *Mus:* Gerard Schurmann. *Exec. prod:*
Anthony Hinds. *Assoc. prod:* Peter Manley. *Prod:*
Michael Carreras. *Rel:* Warner-Pathe (Britain), 20th
Century-Fox (USA). 98 mins. Technicolor.
With Eric Porter (*Capt. Lansen*), Hildegard Knef
(*Eva*), Suzanna Leigh (*Unity*), Tony Beckley
(*Tyler*), Nigel Stock (*Webster*), Neil McCallum
(*Hemmings*), Benito Carruthers (*Ricaldi*), Jimmy
Hanley (*Pat*).

Frankenstein Must be Destroyed (1969)
Dir: Terence Fisher. *Sc:* Bert Batt, from a story by
Anthony Nelson-Keys and Bert Batt. *Ph:* Arthur
Grant. *Art dir:* Bernard Robinson. *Ed:* Gordon
Hales. *Mus:* James Bernard. *Prod:* Anthony

Nelson-Keys. *Rel:* Warner-Pathe (Britain), Warner
Bros.—Seven Arts (USA). 97 mins. Technicolor.
With Peter Cushing (*Baron Frankenstein*), Veronica
Carlson (*Anna Spengler*), Simon Ward (*Karl Holst*),
Freddie Jones (*Professor Richter*), Thorley Walters
(*Inspector Fritsch*), Maxine Audley (*Ella Brandt*).

Moon Zero Two (1969)
A Hammer/Warner Bros.—Seven Arts Production
Dir: Roy Ward Baker. *Sc:* Michael Carreras, from a
story by Gavin Lyall, Frank Hardman, and Martin
Davison. *Ph:* Paul Beeson. *Art dir:* Scott
MacGregor. *Ed:* Spencer Reeve. *Mus:* Don Ellis.
Prod: Michael Carreras. *Rel:* Warner-Pathe
(Britain), Warner Bros.—Seven Arts (USA). 100
mins. Technicolor.
With James Olson (*Bill Kemp*), Catherina von
Schell (*Clementine Taplin*), Warren Mitchell
(*J.J. Hubbard*), Adrienne Corri (*Liz Murphy*), Ori
Levy (*Karminski*), Dudley Foster (*Whitsun*),
Bernard Bresslaw (*Harry*).

Taste the Blood of Dracula (1970)
Dir: Peter Sasdy. *Sc:* John Elder [Anthony Hinds]
based on the character created by Bram Stoker.
Ph: Arthur Grant. *Art dir:* Scott MacGregor. *Ed:*
Chris Barnes. *Mus:* James Bernard. *Prod:* Aida
Young. *Rel:* Warner-Pathe (Britain), Warner
Bros.—Seven Arts (USA). 95 mins. Technicolor.
With Christopher Lee (*Count Dracula*), Geoffrey
Keen (*William Hargood*), Gwen Watford (*Martha
Hargood*), Linda Hayden (*Alice Hargood*), Peter
Sallis (*Samuel Paxton*).

Crescendo (1970)
A Hammer/Warner Bros.—Seven Arts Production
Dir: Alan Gibson. *Sc:* Jimmy Sangster, Alfred
Shaughnessy, from a screenplay by Alfred
Shaughnessy. *Ph:* Paul Beeson. *Art dir:* Scott
MacGregor. *Ed:* Chris Barnes. *Mus:* Malcolm
Williamson. *Prod:* Michael Carreras. *Rel:* Warner-
Pathe (Britain), Warner Bros.—Seven Arts (USA).
95 mins. Technicolor.
With Stefanie Powers (*Susan Roberts*), James
Olson (*Georges/Jacques*), Margaretta Scott
(*Danielle Ryman*), Jane Lapotaire (*Lillianne*), Joss
Ackland (*Carter*), Kirsten Betts (*Catherine*).

Horror of Frankenstein (1970)
Dir: Jimmy Sangster. *Sc:* Jeremy Burnham, Jimmy
Sangster, from the characters created by Mary
Shelley. *Ph:* Moray Grant. *Art dir:* Scott
MacGregor. *Ed:* Chris Barnes. *Mus:* Malcolm
Williamson. *Prod:* Jimmy Sangster. *Rel:* MGM-EMI
(Britain). 95 mins. Technicolor.
With Ralph Bates (*Victor Frankenstein*), Kate
O'Mara (*Alys*), Graham James (*Wilhelm*), Veronica
Carlson (*Elizabeth*), Bernard Archard (*Elizabeth's
father*), Dennis Price (*Grave Robber*), Joan Rice
(*Grave Robber's Wife*), David Prowse (*The
Monster*).

Scars of Dracula (1970)
Dir: Roy Ward Baker. *Sc:* John Elder [Anthony Hinds] from the character created by Bram Stoker. *Ph:* Moray Grant. *Art dir:* Scott MacGregor. *Ed:* James Needs. *Mus:* James Bernard. *Prod:* Aida Young. *Rel:* MGM-EMI (Britain). 96 mins. Technicolor.
With Christopher Lee (*Count Dracula*), Dennis Waterman (*Simon*), Jenny Hanley (*Sarah Framsen*), Christopher Matthews (*Paul*), Patrick Troughton (*Klove*), Michael Gwynn (*Priest*).

When Dinosaurs Ruled the Earth (1970)
Dir: Val Guest. *Sc:* Val Guest, from a treatment by J.G. Ballard. *Ph:* Dick Bush. *Art dir:* John Blezard. *Ed:* Peter Curran. *Mus:* Mario Nascimbene. *Prod:* Aida Young. *Rel:* Warner Bros. 100 mins (Britain), 96 mins (USA). Technicolor.
With Victoria Vetri (*Sanna*), Robin Hawdon (*Tara*), Patrick Allen (*Kingsor*), Drewe Henley (*Khaku*), Sean Caffrey (*Kane*), Magda Konopka (*Ulido*), Imogen Hassall (*Ayak*), Patrick Holt (*Ammon*).

The Vampire Lovers (1970)
A Hammer—American International Production
Dir: Roy Ward Baker. *Sc:* Tudor Gates, from an adaptation by Harry Fine, Tudor Gates and Michael Style of the story "Carmilla" by J. Sheridan Le Fanu. *Ph:* Moray Grant. *Art dir:* Scott MacGregor. *Ed:* James Needs. *Mus:* Harry Robinson. *Prod:* Harry Fine, Michael Style. *Rel:* MGM-EMI (Britain), American International (USA). 91 mins (Britain), 88 mins (USA). Technicolor.
With Ingrid Pitt (*Mircalla/Marcilla/Carmilla*), Pippa Steele (*Laura*), Madeleine Smith (*Emma*), Peter Cushing (*The General*), George Cole (*Morton*), Dawn Addams (*The Countess*), Kate O'Mara (*Governess*), Douglas Wilmer (*Baron Hartog*), Jon Finch (*Carl*), Kirsten Betts, John Forbes Robertson, Harvey Hall.

Lust for a Vampire (1971)
Dir: Jimmy Sangster. *Sc:* Tudor Gates, from characters created by J. Sheridan Le Fanu. *Ph:* David Muir. *Art dir:* Don Mingaye. *Ed:* Spencer Reeve. *Mus:* Harry Robinson. *Prod:* Harry Fine, Michael Style. *Rel:* MGM-EMI (Britain). 95 mins. Technicolor.
With Ralph Bates (*Giles Barton*), Barbara Jefford (*Countess*), Suzanna Leigh (*Janet*), Michael Johnson (*Richard Lestrange*), Yutte Stensgaard (*Mircalla*), Mike Raven (*Count Karnstein*), Helen Christie (*Miss Simpson*), Pippa Steel (*Susan*), David Healy, Michael Brennan, Laun Peters, Christopher Cunningham, Judy Matheson, Caryl Little, Jack Melford, Eric Chitty, Christopher Neame, Harvey Hall.

Countess Dracula (1971)
Dir: Peter Sasdy. *Sc:* Jeremy Paul, from a story by Alexander Paal and Peter Sasdy based on an idea by Gabriel Ronay. *Ph:* Ken Talbot. *Art dir:* Philip Harrison. *Ed:* Henry Richardson. *Mus:* Harry Robinson *Prod:* Alexander Paal. *Rel:* Rank (Britain). 93 mins. Eastman Colour.
With Ingrid Pitt (*Countess Elisabeth Nadasdy*), Nigel Green (*Capt. Dobi*), Sandor Eles (*Imre Toth*), Maurice Denham (*Master Fabio*), Patience Collier (*Julia*), Peter Jeffrey (*Captain Balogh*), Lesley-Anne Down (*Ilona*).

Creatures the World Forgot (1971)
Dir: Don Chaffey. *Sc:* Michael Carreras. *Ph:* Vincent Cox. *Prod. des:* John Stoll. *Ed:* Chris Barnes. *Mus:* Mario Nascimbene. *Prod:* Michael Carreras. *Rel:* Columbia. 95 mins. Technicolor.
With Julie Ege (*Nala*), Brian O'Shaughnessy (*Mak*), Tony Bonner (*Toomak*), Robert John (*Rool*).

On the Buses (1971)
Dir: Harry Booth. *Sc:* Ronald Wolfe, Ronald Chesney, from the TV series. *Ph:* Mark McDonald. *Prod. des:* Scott MacGregor. *Ed:* Archie Ludski. *Mus:* Max Harris. *Prod:* Ronald Wolfe, Ronald Chesney. *Rel:* MGM-EMI (Britain). 88 mins. Technicolor.
With Reg Varney (*Stan Butler*), Doris Hare (*Stan's Mum*), Michael Robbins (*Arthur*), Anna Karen (*Olive*), Stephen Lewis (*Blakey*), Bob Grant (*Jack*), Andrea Lawrence (*Betty*), Pat Ashton (*Sally*), Brian Oulton (*Manager*), Pamela Cundell (*Ruby*), Pat Coombs (*Vera*).

Hands of the Ripper (1971)
Dir: Peter Sasdy. *Sc:* L. W. Davidson, from a story by Edward Spencer Shew. *Ph:* Kenneth Talbot. *Art dir:* Roy Stannard. *Ed:* Christopher Barnes. *Mus:* Christopher Gunning. *Prod:* Aida Young. *Rel:* Rank (Britain). 85 mins. Technicolor.
With Eric Porter (*Dr. John Pritchard*), Angharad Rees (*Anna*), Jane Merrow (*Laura*), Keith Bell (*Michael Pritchard*), Derek Godfrey (*Dysart*), Dora Bryan (*Mrs. Golding*), Marjorie Rhodes (*Mrs. Bryant*).

Twins Of Evil (1971)
Dir: John Hough. *Sc:* Tudor Gates, from characters created by J. Sheridan Le Fanu. *Ph:* Dick Bush. *Art dir:* Roy Stannard. *Ed:* Spencer Reeve. *Mus:* Harry Robinson. *Prod:* Harry Fine, Michael Style. *Rel:* Rank (Britain). 87 mins. Eastman Colour.
With Madeleine Collinson (*Frieda Gellhorn*), Mary Collinson (*Maria Gellhorn*), Peter Cushing (*Gustav Weil*), Kathleen Byron (*Katy Weil*), Dennis Price (*Dietrich*), Harvey Hall (*Franz*), Isobel Black (*Ingrid Hoffer*), Damien Thomas (*Count Karnstein*), David Warbeck (*Anton Hoffer*), Alex Scott (*Hermann*), Katya Keith (*Countess Mircalla*), Roy Stewart (*Joachim*).

Dr. Jekyll & Sister Hyde (1971)
Dir: Roy Ward Baker. *Sc:* Brian Clemens. *Ph:*

Norman Warwick. *Prod. des:* Robert Jones. *Ed:* James Needs. *Mus:* David Whitaker. *Prod:* Albert Fennell, Brian Clemens. *Rel:* MGM-EMI (Britain). 97 mins. Technicolor.
With Ralph Bates (*Dr. Jekyll*), Martine Beswick (*Sister Hyde*), Gerald Sim (*Prof. Robertson*), Lewis Fiander (*Howard*), Dorothy Alison (*Mrs. Spencer*), Ivor Dean (*Burke*), Tony Calvin (*Hare*), Neil Wilson (*Older Policeman*), Paul Whitsun-Jones (*Sgt. Danvers*), Philip Madoc (*Byker*).

Blood from the Mummy's Tomb (1971)
Dir: Seth Holt, Michael Carreras*. *Sc:* Christopher Wicking, from the novel *Jewel of the Seven Stars* by Bram Stoker. *Ph:* Arthur Grant. *Art dir:* Scott MacGregor. *Ed:* Peter Weatherley. *Mus:* Tristram Cary. *Prod:* Howard Brandy. *Rel:* MGM-EMI (Britain). 94 mins. Technicolor.
With Andrew Keir (*Prof. Julian Fuchs*), Valerie Leon (*Margaret/Tera*), James Villiers (*Corbeck*), Hugh Burden (*Dandridge*), George Coulouris (*Berigan*), Mark Edwards (*Tod Browning*), Rosalie Crutchley (*Helen Dickerson*), Aubrey Morris (*Dr. Putnam*), David Markham (*Dr. Burgess*), Joan Young (*Mrs. Caporal*).

*The film's last few days of shooting were undertaken by Carreras on the death of Seth Holt.

Vampire Circus (1972)
Dir: Robert Young. *Sc:* Judson Kinberg, from a story by George Baxt and Wilbur Stark. *Ph:* Moray Grant. *Art dir:* Scott MacGregor. *Ed:* Peter Musgrave. *Mus:* David Whittaker. *Prod:* Wilbur Stark. *Rel:* Rank (Britain), 20th Century-Fox (USA). 87 mins. Colour.
With Adrienne Corri (*Gypsy Woman*), Laurence Payne (*Mueller*), Thorley Walters (*Burgermeister*), John Moulder Brown (*Anton Kersh*), Lynne Frederick (*Dora Mueller*), Elizabeth Seal (*Gerta Hauser*), Anthony Corlan (*Emil*), Richard Owens (*Dr. Kersh*), Domini Blythe (*Anna Mueller*), Robin Hunter (*Hauser*).

Fear in the Night (1972)
Dir: Jimmy Sangster. *Sc:* Jimmy Sangster, Michael Syson. *Ph:* Arthur Grant. *Art dir:* Don Picton. *Ed:* Peter Weatherley. *Mus:* John McCabe. *Exec. prod:* Michael Carreras. *Prod:* Jimmy Sangster. *Rel:* MGM-EMI (Britain). 86 mins. Technicolor.
With Judy Geeson (*Peggy Heller*), Joan Collins (*Molly Carmichael*), Ralph Bates (*Robert Heller*), Peter Cushing (*Michael Carmichael*), Gillian Lind (*Mrs. Beamish*), James Cossins (*Doctor*), John Bown, Brian Grellis.

Straight On Till Morning (1972)
Dir: Peter Collinson. *Sc:* Michael Peacock. *Ph:* Brian Probyn. *Art dir:* Scott MacGregor. *Ed:* Alan Pattillo. *Mus:* Roland Shaw. *Exec. prod:* Michael Carreras. *Rel:* MGM-EMI (Britain). 96 mins. Technicolor.
With Rita Tushingham (*Brenda Thompson*), Shane Briant (*Peter*), Tom Bell (*Jimmy Lindsay*), Annie Ross (*Liza*), Katya Wyeth (*Caroline*), James Bolam (*Joey*), Clare Kelly (*Margo*), Harold Berens (*Mr. Harris*).

Mutiny on the Buses (1972)
Dir: Harry Booth. *Sc:* Ronald Wolfe, Ronald Chesney, from their TV series. *Ph:* Mark McDonald. *Art dir:* Scott MacGregor. *Ed:* Archie Ludski. *Mus:* Ron Grainer. *Prod:* Ronald Wolfe, Ronald Chesney. *Rel:* MGM-EMI (Britain). 89 mins. Technicolor.
With Reg Varney (*Stan Butler*), Doris Hare (*Mrs. Butler*), Anna Karen (*Olive*), Michael Robbins (*Arthur*), Bob Grant (*Jack*), Stephen Lewis (*Inspector Blake*), Pat Ashton (*Norah*), Janet Mahoney (*Susy*), Caroline Dowdeswell (*Sandra*), Kevin Brennan (*Mr. Jenkins*).

Demons of the Mind (1972)
A Hammer—Frank Godwin Production
Dir: Peter Sykes. *Sc:* Christopher Wicking, from a story by Christopher Wicking and Frank Godwin. *Ph:* Arthur Grant. *Art dir:* Michael Stringer. *Ed:* Chris Barnes. *Mus:* Harry Robinson. *Prod:* Frank Godwin. *Rel:* MGM-EMI (Britain). 89 mins. Technicolor.
With Paul Jones (*Carl Richter*), Gillian Hills (*Elizabeth Zorn*), Robert Hardy (*Baron Friedrich Zorn*), Michael Hordern (*Priest*), Patrick Magee (*Dr. Falkenberg*), Shane Briant (*Emil Zorn*), Yvonne Mitchell (*Aunt Hilda*), Kenneth J. Warren (*Klaus*), Robert Brown (*Fischinger*).

Dracula A.D.1972 (1972)
Dir: Alan Gibson. *Sc:* Don Houghton. *Ph:* Dick Bush. *Prod. des:* Don Mingaye. *Ed:* James Needs. *Mus:* Michael Vickers. *Prod:* Josephine Douglas. *Rel:* Warner Bros. (Britain, through Columbia-Warner). 97 mins. Eastman Colour.
With Christopher Lee (*Count Dracula*), Peter Cushing (*Prof. Van Helsing*), Stephanie Beacham (*Jessica Van Helsing*), Michael Coles (*Inspector*), Christopher Neame (*Johnny Alucard*), William Ellis (*Joe Mitchum*), Marsha Hunt (*Gaynor*), Janet Key (*Anna*), Philip Miller (*Bob*), Michael Kitchen (*Greg*).

The Satanic Rites of Dracula (1973)
Dir: Alan Gibson. *Sc:* Don Houghton. *Ph:* Brian Probyn. *Art dir:* Lionel Couch. *Ed:* Christopher Barnes. *Prod:* Roy Skeggs. *Rel:* Warner Bros. (Britain, through Columbia-Warner). Colour.
With Christopher Lee (*Count Dracula*), Peter Cushing (*Van Helsing*), William Franklyn (*Torrence*), Michael Coles (*Inspector Murray*), Joanna Lumley (*Jessica*), Freddie Jones (*Prof. Keeley*), Barbara Yu Ling (*Chin Yang*), Valerie Ost (*Jane*), Richard Vernon (*Col. Mathews*).

That's Your Funeral (1973)
Dir: John Robins. *Sc:* Peter Lewis. *Ph:* David Holmes. *Art dir:* Scott MacGregor. *Ed:* Archie Ludski. *Prod:* Michael Carreras. *Rel:* Rank (Britain, through Fox-Rank). Colour. 82 mins.
With Bill Fraser (*Basil Bulstrode*), Raymond Huntley (*Emanuel Holroyd*), David Battley (*Percy*), John Ronane (*Mr. Smallbody*), Dennis Price (*Mr. Soul*), Sue Lloyd (*Miss Peach*), Richard Wattis (*Simmonds*), Roy Kinnear (*Mr. Purvis*).

Frankenstein and the Monster from Hell (1973)
Dir: Terence Fisher. *Sc:* John Elder [Anthony Hinds]. *Ph:* Brian Probyn. *Art dir:* Scott MacGregor. *Ed:* James Needs. *Prod:* Roy Skeggs. *Rel:* Paramount (USA). Colour.
With Peter Cushing (*Baron Frankenstein*), Shane Briant (*Dr. Helder*), Madeline Smith (*The Angel/Sarah*), John Stratton (*The Director*), Bernard Lee (*Tarmut*), Clifford Mollison (*Judge*), Dave Prowse (*The Monster*), Patrick Troughton (*Body Snatcher*).

Kronos (1973)
Dir: Brian Clemens. *Sc:* Brian Clemens. *Ph:* Ian Wilson. *Prod. des:* Robert Jones. *Ed:* James Needs. *Prod:* Albert Fennell, Brian Clemens. Colour.
With Horst Janson (*Kronos*), John Carson (*Doctor Marcus*), John Cater (*Professor Grost*), Shane Briant (*Paul Durward*), Caroline Munro (*Carla*), Ian Hendry (*Kerro*), Wanda Ventham (*Lady Durward*), Lois Daine (*Sara Durward*), William Hobbs (*Hagen*).

Love Thy Neighbour (1973)
Dir: John Robins. *Sc:* Vince Powell, Harry Driver, from their TV series. *Ph:* Moray Grant. *Art dir:* Lionel Couch. *Ed:* James Needs. *Prod:* Roy Skeggs. *Rel:* MGM-EMI (Britain). Colour.
With Jack Smethurst (*Eddie Booth*), Rudolph Walker (*Bill*), Nina Baden-Semper (*Barbie*), Kate Williams (*Joan*).

Nearest and Dearest (1973)
A Hammer—Granada Production
Dir: John Robins. *Sc:* Tom Brennand, Roy Bottomley, from the TV series. *Ph:* David Holmes. *Art dir:* Scott Macgregor. *Prod:* Michael Carreras. Colour.
With Hylda Baker, Jimmy Jewel, Joe Gladwin, Eddie Malin, Madge Hindle.

Man at the Top (1973)
A Hammer—Dufton Production
Dir: Mike Vardy. *Sc:* Hugh Whitemore, from the TV series based on characters in the book "Room at the Top" by John Braine. *Ph:* Brian Probyn. *Art dir:* Don Picton. *Ed:* Christopher Barnes. *Exec. prod:* Roy Skeggs. *Prod:* Peter Charlesworth, Jock Jacobsen. *Rel:* MGM-EMI (Britain). Colour. Wide screen.
With Kenneth Haigh (*Joe Lampton*), Nanette Newman (*Lady Ackerman — Alex*), Harry Andrews (*Lord Ackerman*), William Lucas (*Marshall*), Clive Swift (*Massey*), Paul Williamson (*Tarrant*), John Collin (*Wisbech*), John Quentin (*Digby*), Danny Sewell (*Weston*), Charlie Williams (*George Harvey*), Anne Cunningham (*Mrs. Harvey*), Angela Bruce (*Joyce*), Margaret Heald (*Eileen*), Jaron Yaltan (*Taranath*), Tim Brinton (*Newsreader*), Norma West (*Sarah Tarrant*).

Frankenstein and the Monster from Hell: David Prowse

Man About the House (1974)
Dir: John Robins. *Sc:* Johnnie Mortimer,
Brian Cooke. *Ph:* Jimmy Allen. *Art dir:* Don
Picton. *Ed:* Archie Ludski. *Prod:* Roy Skeggs.
Rel: EMI. Colour.
With Richard O'Sullivan *(Robin Tripp)*,
Paula Wilcox *(Chrissy)*, Sally Thomsett *(Jo)*,
Brian Murphy *(Mr Roper)*, Yootha Joyce
(Mrs Roper), Doug Fisher *(Larry Simmonds)*,
Peter Cellier *(Morris Pluthero)*, Patrick
Newell *(Sir Edmund Weir)*, Aimi McDonald
(Hazel Lovett), Jack Smethurst *(Himself)*,
Rudolph Walker *(Himself)*, Spike Milligan
(Himself), Melvyn Hayes *(Nigel)*, Michael
Ward *(Mr Gideon)*, Bill Grundy *(Interviewer)*.

The Legend of the 7 Golden Vampires (1974)
A Hammer (London)/Shaw Brothers (Hong
Kong) Production. *Dir:* Roy Ward Baker.
Sc: Don Houghton. *Ph:* John Wilcox, Roy
Ford. *Art dir:* Johnson Tsao. *Sp Effects:* Les
Bowie. *Ed:* Chris Barnes. *Prod:* Don
Houghton, Vee King Shaw. *Exec Prod:*
Michael Carreras, Run Run Shaw. *Rel:*
Columbia-Warner. Colour.
With Peter Cushing *(Professor Lawrence Van
Helsing)*, David Chiang *(Hsi Ching)*, Julie
Ege *(Vanessa Buren)*, Robin Stewart *(Leyland
Van Helsing)*, Shih Szu *(Mai Kwei)*, John
Forbes-Robertson *(Dracula)*, Robert Hanna
(British Consul), Chan Shen *(Kah)*, James Ma
(Hsi Ta), Liu Chia Yung *(Hsi Kwei)*, Feng Ko
An *(Hsi Sung)*, Chen Tien Loong *(Hsi San)*,
Wong Han Chan *(Leung Hon)*.

Shatter (1974)
A Hammer (London)/Shaw Brothers (Hong
Kong) Production. *Dir:* Michael Carreras.
Sc: Don Houghton. *Ph:* Brian Probyn, John
Wilcox, Roy Ford. *Art dir:* Johnson Tsao.
Sp Effects: Les Bowie. *Ed:* Eric Boyd-
Perkins. *Prod:* Michael Carreras, Vee King
Shaw.
With Stuart Whitman *(Shatter)*, Ti Lung *(Tai
Pah)*, Lily Li [Li Li-Li] *(Mai Ling)*, Peter
Cushing *(Rattwood)*, Anton Diffring *(Hans
Leber)*, Yemi Ajibade *(Ansabi M'Goya/
Dabula M'Goya)*, Liu Ka-Yong and Huang
Pei-Chi *(Bodyguards)*, Liu Ya-Ying *(Leber's
Girl)*, Lo Wei *(Howe)*, James Ma *(Thai Boxer)*,
Chiang Han *(Korean Boxer)*, Kao Hsiung
(Japanese Boxer).

To the Devil a Daughter (1976)
A Hammer (London)/Terra Filmkunst (West
Germany) Production. *Dir:* Peter Sykes.
Sc: Chris Wicking. Based on the novel by
Dennis Wheatley. *Ph:* David Watkin. *Art dir:*
Don Picton. *Sp Effects:* Les Bowie. *Ed:* John
Trumper. *Prod:* Roy Skeggs.
With Richard Widmark *(John Verney)*,
Christopher Lee *(Father Michael Rayner)*,
Honor Blackman *(Anna Fountain)*, Denholm
Elliott *(Henry Beddows)*, Michael Goodliffe
(George De Grass), Nastassja Kinski
(Catherine), Eva Maria Meineke *(Eveline De
Grass)*, Anthony Valentine *(David)*, Derek
Francis *(Bishop)*, Isabella Telezynska
(Margaret), Constantin De Goguel *(Kollde)*,
Anna Bentinck *(Isabel)*.

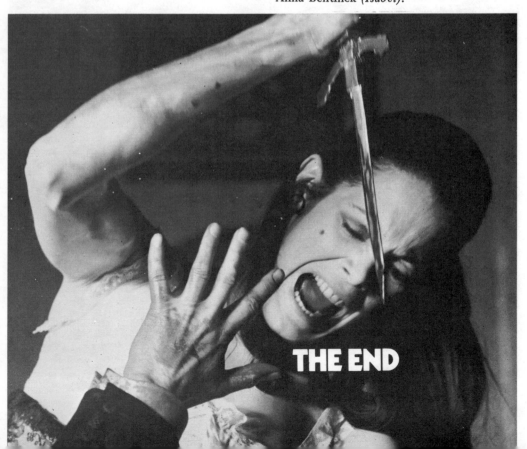

THE END

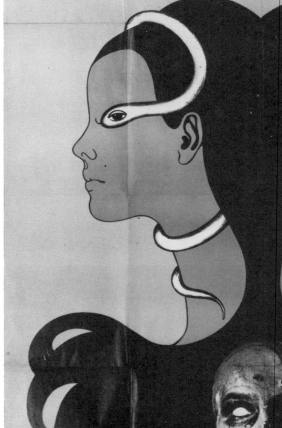

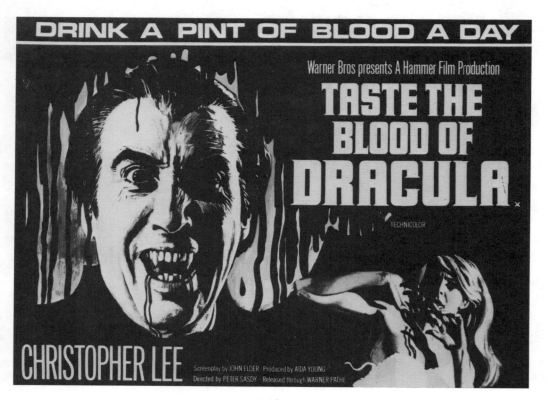

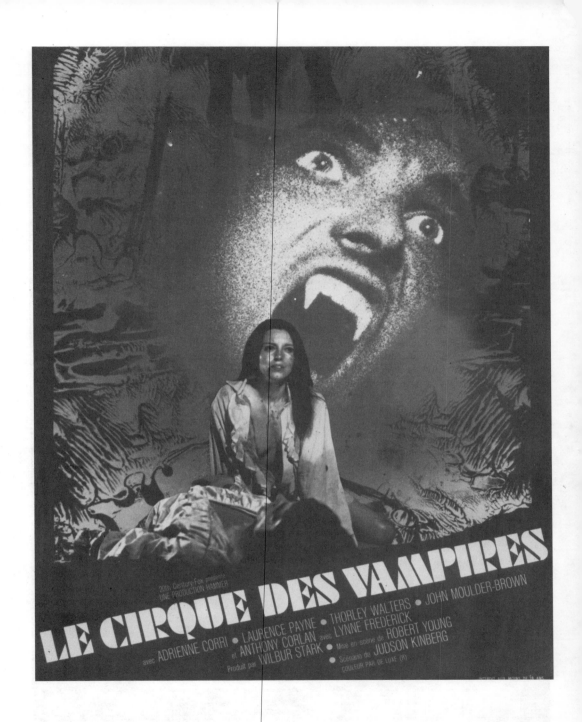

LE CIRQUE DES VAMPIRES

20th Century-Fox présente
UNE PRODUCTION HAMMER

avec ADRIENNE CORRI • LAURENCE PAYNE • THORLEY WALTERS • JOHN MOULDER-BROWN
et ANTHONY CORLAN avec LYNNE FREDERICK
Produit par WILBUR STARK • Mise en scène de ROBERT YOUNG
• Scénario de JUDSON KINBERG
COULEUR PAR DE LUXE (R)

INTERDIT AUX MOINS DE 18 ANS

UNE MESSE POUR DRACULA

CHRISTOPHER LEE   LINDA HAYDEN   ANTHONY CORLAN